Translation, Power, Subversion

TOPICS IN TRANSLATION

Series Editors: Susan Bassnett (*University of Warwick*)
and André Lefevere (*University of Texas, Austin*)

Editor for Annotated Texts for Translation: Beverly Adab (*Aston University, Birmingham*)

Editor for Translation in the Commercial Environment:
Geoffrey Samuelsson-Brown (*Aardvark Translation Services Ltd*)

Other Books in the Series

Annotated Texts for Translation: French – English
    BEVERLY ADAB
Annotated Texts for Translation: English – French
    BEVERLY ADAB
Linguistic Auditing
    NIGEL REEVES and COLIN WRIGHT
Paragraphs on Translation
    PETER NEWMARK
Practical Guide for Translators
    GEOFFREY SAMUELSSON-BROWN
The Coming Industry of Teletranslation
    MINAKO O'HAGAN

Other Books of Interest

About Translation
    PETER NEWMARK
Cultural Functions of Translation
    C. SCHÄFFNER and H. KELLY-HOLMES (eds)

Please contact us for the latest book information:
Multilingual Matters Ltd, Frankfurt Lodge, Clevedon Hall,
Victoria Road, Clevedon BS21 7SJ, England

TOPICS IN TRANSLATION 8
Series Editors: Susan Bassnett (*University of Warwick*) and
André Lefevere (*University of Texas, Austin*)

Translation, Power, Subversion

Edited by

Román Álvarez and M. Carmen-África Vidal

MULTILINGUAL MATTERS LTD
Clevedon • Philadelphia • Adelaide

Library of Congress Cataloging in Publication Data

Translation, Power, Subversion/Edited by Román Álvarez and M. Carmen África
Topics in Translation: 8
Includes bibliographical references.
1. Translating and interpreting–Social aspects. I. Alvarez, Román. II. Vidal, M.
Carmen África. III. Series.
P306.2.T739   1996
418'.02–dc20   95-50708

British Library Cataloguing in Publication Data

A CIP catalogue record for this book is available from the British Library.

ISBN 1-85359-351-6 (hbk)
ISBN 1-85359-350-8 (pbk)

Multilingual Matters Ltd

UK: Frankfurt Lodge, Clevedon Hall, Victoria Road, Clevedon BS21 7SJ.
USA: 1900 Frost Road, Suite 101, Bristol, PA 19007, USA.
Australia: P.O. Box 6025, 95 Gilles Street, Adelaide, SA 5000, Australia.

Copyright © 1996 Román Álvarez and M. Carmen-África Vidal

Typeset by Bookcraft, Stroud, Glos.
Printed and bound in Great Britain by WBC Book Manufacturers Ltd.

Contents

Acknowledgements

The editors would like to express their gratitude to all the contributors in this book for their work, support and encouragement. Special thanks should be extended to Professors Susan Bassnett and André Lefevere for their sustained help with this project over the last two years, and for the much valuable criticism and advice they gave us. We are also grateful to Prof. Fernando Toda, who held the first chair in the area of Translation Studies in Spain at the University of Salamanca, for his lucid and perceptive comments on the contents of the book. The editors would also like to acknowledge their great indebtedness to Prof. Ramón López Ortega, whose annual Symposia on Translation at the University of Extremadura, attended by thousands of translators, teachers and students, did a great deal to develop the interest in this area in Spain.

R.A. and M.C.A.V.

1 Translating: A Political Act

ROMÁN ÁLVAREZ AND M. CARMEN-ÁFRICA VIDAL

> *Translation, as scholarship (to which it is integral), is a constant forward movement of approach to another cultural space. A constant movement, because real knowledge of the other culture is never achieved, be it at the linguistic or semiotic level. And a forward movement, because it implies a goal, the consecution of sufficient data of an ideal, abstract space which is linked with the progressive advance of the civilizational frontier. Any other space is therefore a shifty signified.*
>
> Lawrence Venuti

It could be said that throughout the second half of the twentieth century Translation Studies have evolved on the par with the changes and development of Western society and have been a reflection of them. As communications made the world smaller every day, the translator became more and more of a necessity. From the eagerness to consider translation as a science or the obsession to give a definitive, prescriptive and sole version of a text, we have moved on to a descriptive outlook which likewise, whether we like it or not, is political. As Susan Bassnett states in her essay in this book, at the end of the twentieth century the attitude towards translation has radically changed: 'Globally, this is the age of mass communications, of multi-media experiences and a world where audiences demand to share the latest text, be it film, song, or book simultaneously across cultures. Nor has the development of English as a world language slowed down the process of translation; it has, on the contrary served to emphasize the significance of translation, as questions of cultural politics appear on the agenda . . . the study and practice of translation is inevitably an exploration of power relationships within textual practice that reflect power structures within the wider cultural context.'

1

Translation has been one of the most representative paradigms of the clash between two cultures. Although excellent studies already exist on this function of translation – particularly stemming from the so-called 'Manipulation School' – there remains much work to be done with regard to the semiotic and hermeneutic problems translation poses. Contemporary studies on translation are aware of the need to examine in depth the relationship between the production of knowledge in a given culture and its transmission, relocation, and reinterpretation in the target culture. This obviously has to do with the production and ostentation of power and with the strategies used by this power in order to represent the other culture. Translation is *culture bound*. It makes us ponder, as Edward Said would put it, how knowledge that is non-dominative and non-coercive can be produced in a setting that is deeply inscribed with the politics, the considerations, the positions and the strategies of power. The translator can artificially create the reception context of a given text. He can be the authority who manipulates the culture, politics, literature, and their acceptance (or lack thereof) in the target culture. He may stay 'behind the language of the original with its local densities, idiomatic variables, and historical-stylistic accidence'. The translator views his source 'often via an intermediate paraphrase, as a feature, almost non-linguistic, of landscape, reported custom, and simplified history'.[1] He knows that:

> To experience difference, to feel the characteristic resistance and 'materiality' of that which differs, is to re-experience identity. One's own space is mapped by what lies outside; it derives coherence, tactile configuration, from the pressure of the external. 'Otherness', particularly when it has the wealth and penetration of language, compels 'presentness' to stand clear.[2]

Therefore, he should 'situate precisely and convey intact the "otherness" of the original',[3] but his knowledge of the target culture may not be used objectively. On the contrary, he may be influenced by the relationships of power that his culture maintains with the target culture. Obviously, cultural hegemony plays an important role in translation:[4] '. . . an account of the accumulation of knowledge by one people about another is most unlikely to be the record of a progressive revelation of objective truth, achieved through the disinterested quest of learning for its own sake.'[5] As Theo Hermans argues in his essay, translating is a matter of adjusting and manipulating a ST so as to bring the TT into line with a particular model and hence a particular correctness notion, and in so doing to secure social acceptance, even acclaim.

Approaching a culture inexorably implies beginning a process of translation. It is not merely a question of there being diverse institutional and cultural terms which pose evident translation problems[6]. Sometimes there is a void because something does not exist in the other culture or because it has a very different meaning or value (thus, the well-known example of 'Lamb of God' in the case of the Eskimos). In order for translation to exist, there must have been not only a perfect assimilation of the linguistic content, but also of the experience of the other culture, without the pressures of one 'superior' culture over another. As it is approached today, translation tackles some of the most important cultural problems: the death of what Lyotard has called the *'Grand Récits'*; the consequences of colonization in the interpretation of other cultures; the problems springing from the rebirth of xenophobia and racism; the understanding of the exotic, not in terms of false imaginary constructions, but as an historic reality in itself which must be respected disregarding hierarchical cultural boundaries. It could be said that translation is a provisional way to encounter the strangeness of languages, to paraphrase Benjamin, although it can also become a form of control, particularly if there are already a series of preconceived stereotypes about a given culture.

A characteristic example might be the translation of post-colonial literature – 'hybrid,' or 'métisse'[7] – in which the exotic discourse can be manipulated to such an extent as to conceive it, Edward Said argues,[8] as an invented geography, an imaginary space built according to the ideology, cultural values and norms of the West – the Oriental orientalized – something as it should have been but not what it in fact is. When translating, one ego can be idealized, e.g. by selecting the vocabulary over another, by placing more emphasis on the familiar part of that culture or on its most exotic side; on that which makes us closer to it or 'superior': 'exotism' as opposed to 'naturalism'.[9]

It is no longer possible, therefore, to speak of a textual translation; rather, the context should always be born in mind because 'the opposition between "a contextual interpretation" and one that is not contextual is entirely spurious. Nothing has meaning "in isolation." The problem is always, what kind of context?'[10] The problem is, indeed, what kind of context? Who chooses it? Why and how was it chosen? The answers to these questions have even changed many of the accepted ideas of translation theory.[11]

The importance of the cultural milieu of each language is such that it could be argued that its significance cannot be found at a linguistic level (neither SL nor TL) but rather on a third level: in the cultural space that emerges from the clash (although, ideally, intersection) between the two cultures; a cultural space that is usually as complex as it is conflicting. Translation is 'an integral part of the reading experience'.[12]

In these cases, the translator can become a true author, by determining what the implicit meanings of the final version are and also those of the original version: 'If the anthropological translator, like the analyst, has final authority in determining the subject's meanings – it is then the former who becomes *the real author* of the latter. In this view, "cultural translation" is a matter of determining implicit meanings'.[13] For example, in *Se una notte d'inverno un viaggiatore* . . . the protagonist is a translator, Ermes Marana, who adulterates the translations as he pleases, manipulating the original texts. One of the assignments he is given has political implications. The young wife of a sultan married him on the condition that she would always be provided with the latest books written in Western countries, which she could read with ease. However, he begins to suspect that the guidelines for the beginnings of a revolution were being surreptitiously introduced between the lines of these novels since the sultana could not be deprived of them. The sultan knew that the conspirators where waiting for a signal from the sultana to begin, but that she had ordered no one to bother her while she was reading. In the light of this situation the translator, Ermes Marana, comes up with a strategy: the manipulation of the original text through translation with political ends. Therefore,

> . . . he will interrupt the translation at one of its most gripping points and he will begin to translate another novel, inserting it into the first by any rudimentary means; for example, a character of the first novel opens a book and begins to read . . . Also, the second novel will be interrupted to make room for a third, which will not go far before it gives way to a fourth, and so on . . . Ermes Marana is like a snake that worms his evil way into the paradise of the prose . . . Here is a novel-cum-snare set by the disloyal translator with the beginnings of a novel left hanging . . . Like the rebellion, also left hanging, while the conspirators wait in vain to communicate with their illustrious accomplice . . .[14]

Translation always implies an unstable balance between the power one culture can exert over another. Translation is not the production of one text equivalent to another text, but rather a complex process of rewriting that runs parallel both to the overall view of language and of the 'Other' people have throughout history; and to the influences and the balance of power that exist between one culture and another. As Javier Franco states in his article, when translating we are confronted with four basic types of problems: linguistic, interpretive (those who have denied the possibility that translation could become a science), pragmatic or intertextual (based on conventions of expression for each type of discourse, which are different for each society), and cultural (with its variant of historical distance). Every linguistic community also has its own set of values, norms, and classification systems which at times will differ from those of the target culture, and coincide with them at other times. According to Franco, this creates a factor of variability which the translator must somehow resolve, from the conservation and acceptance of the difference ('reading as an original,' as Toury calls it) to naturalization (which makes the other an equal), depending on the degree of tolerance.

Therefore, the translator's conduct will never be innocent and can lead to 'a labor of acculturation which domesticates the foreign text, making it intelligible and even familiar to the target-language reader, providing him or her with the narcissistic experience of recognizing his or her own cultural other'.[15] Translation creates an image of the original, particularly for those who have no access to the reality of that original. This image can undoubtedly be very different from the truth, insofar as the translator can distort and manipulate reality, because he is under the pressure of a series of constraints (which Lefevere denotes as ideological, poetical and economic), typical of the culture to which he belongs.

Therefore it is important to acknowledge the consequences of manipulating the language and the problem of abuse of power that translation can give rise to. From all this, the importance of knowing what is being rewritten and how it is rewritten stands out[16] (what is translated; what is included in literary anthologies; what is taught in the history of literature), insofar as the idea that the non-professional reader of a given culture will form will be that provided by literary critics, translators and compilers. One must be on one's guard as, according to Lefevere, all rewriting implies manipulation, whether conscious or unconscious, of the original.[17]

If we are aware that translating is not merely passing from one text to another, transferring words from one container to another, but rather transporting one entire culture to another with all that this entails, we realize just how important it is to be conscious of the ideology that underlies a translation. It is essential to know what the translator has added, what he has left out, the words he has chosen, and how he has placed them. Because behind every one of his selections there is a voluntary act that reveals his history and the socio-political milieu that surrounds him; in other words, his own culture.

Translation is an excellent vehicle for conveying the typically Foucaultian binary essence of the opposition power/knowledge: power is intimately related to knowledge, information, and especially to the manner in which that information is conveyed and the way of articulating a wide range of discursive elements in the TT which behave according to extremely subtle strategies.

At a historical period characterized by manipulation, as Robert Scholes states in *Textual Power*, one must ask oneself – in a Foucaultian manner – what is so dangerous about the fact that people speak and that their discourse proliferates indefinitely. It is important to be aware of this manipulation and to try 'to see through the manipulations of all sorts of texts in all sorts of media'[18] as far as possible. One should be aware that 'translating aspects of one culture into another is never a simple semantic substitution. Rather, the self-images of two cultures come to bear on the matter and clash over it . . . Translations, therefore, can teach us much about certain aspects of a culture at certain stages of its evolution'.[19]

Translators are constrained in many ways: by their own ideology; by their feelings of superiority or inferiority towards the language in which they are writing the text being translated; by the prevailing poetical rules at that time; by the very language in which the texts they are translating is written; by what the dominant institutions and ideology expect of them; by the public for whom the translation is intended. The translation itself will depend upon all of these factors.

The essays compiled for this book deal with all of these aspects and many more. Susan Bassnett, for example, gives a retrospective view of the figure of the translator who has been so mistreated over the centuries. As opposed to the old idea of 'the translator as a betrayer of the pure source text', recent translation theory 'has stressed the vital role of the translator in the interpretative process.' The translator is essential during the process of exchange and interchange that takes place when translating. With the author, the original also dies. With the appearance of polysystem theory, translation takes on a principal role in shaping the literary polysystem and assumes an important subversive power which can be illustrated by examples of translations of the Bible and in texts related to post-colonialism and feminism. One must bear in mind 'how the translation ensures the continuity of the source text, in direct contrast to the old notion of the translation as a diminution of the source, or betrayal of it. Translation therefore becomes the act that ensures the life of the text and guarantees its survival. Far from traducing the pure original, the translation injects new life blood into a text bringing it to the attention of a new world of readers in a different language.' According to Bassnett, the key word in the

90s is 'visibility.' Today translation is a process in which intervention is crucial; the role of the translator is 'very visible indeed.'

Theo Hermans writes on the social aspects of translation norms. Starting from the observation that norms are social as well as psychological realities, his essay goes on to discuss norms as part and parcel of the power structures in societies. Individuals or groups may, depending on their position in the system and the goals they wish to achieve, follow dominant norms or deviate from them, or attempt to subvert them. Norms are particularly relevant to translation, as they show how a culture, or elements within it, regulate both the import and export of cultural goods.

In his study, Javier Franco concentrates, from a descriptive point of view, on the nature of culture-specific items in translation and applies his approach to a study of their manipulation in several translations into Spanish of *The Maltese Falcon*. Ovidio Carbonell analyses the question of the 'Other' in connection with translation, with special reference to Islam. Enrique Alcaraz writes on Pragmatics and Translation from the perspective of linguistic manipulation. Edwin Gentzler is involved with Michel de Certeau's ideas about the 'practice' of everyday life and their viability as a model for locating the subversive aspect of translations in the larger framework of social interaction. He gives examples from both Merwin's translations of early Spanish ballads and Bly's translations of poets such as Neruda, Machado and Jiménez, arriving at the conclusion that in these cases they demonstrate that at times the 'weak' culture can influence the 'strong' one. Finally, André Lefevere ponders how translation influences and has influenced the construction of a literary canon, using examples from the corpus of drama anthologies published in the US between 1900 and 1988.

What all of these essays seem to have in common is an approach to translation as a factor that shapes the way in which a given society receives a work, an author, a literature, or a culture: '... like all (re)writings,' Bassnett and Lefevere state in *Translation, History and Culture*, '[translation] is never innocent. There is always a context in which the translation takes place, always a history from which a text emerges and into which a text is transposed.' It is no longer possible to limit oneself to the word as a translation unit; one must take into consideration both the original and target cultures with which the translator is connected. He must be aware that all use of language implies manipulation and that therefore the result of this action could either be a Barthesian 'encratic' discourse (which proliferates within the power) or and 'acratic' one (which proliferates outside of it). The important thing is to confirm the tolerance of the language of the translator when assimilating the 'Other'. We must analyse 'how power enters into the process of "cultural translation," seen both as a discursive and as a non-discursive practice'.[20] It is a question of making clear that the subject who speaks and translates is not as responsible for what he or she says as for *what s/he does not say* and *how s/he says it*.

Notes

1. George Steiner, *After Babel. Aspects of Language and Translation* (New York: Oxford University Press, 1976 [1975]), p. 380. For a critique of Steiner's point, see Samia Mehrez, 'Translation and the Postcolonial Experience: The Franco-phone North African Text,' in Lawrence Venuti (ed.), *Rethinking Translation. Discourse, Subjectivity, Ideology* (London: Routledge, 1993), p. 121.
2. Steiner, *op. cit.*, p. 381.
3. *Ibid.*, p. 413.
4. Cf. Richard Jacquemond, 'Translation and Cultural Hegemony,' in Lawrence Venuti (ed.), *Rethinking Translation. Discourse, Subjectivity, Ideology*, pp. 139–158.
5. P.J. Marshall, 'Taming the Exotic: The British and India in the Seventeenth and Eighteenth Centuries,' in G.S. Rousseau and Roy Porter (eds), *Exoticism in the Enlightenment* (Manchester: Manchester University Press, 1990), p. 52.
6. Cf. Peter Newmark, *Approaches to Translation* (Oxford: Pergamon Press, 1981), pp. 70–83.
7. So called 'because of the culturo-linguistic layering which exists within them.' This kind of literature has managed to create 'a new language that defies the very notion of a "foreign" text that can be readily translatable into another language. With this literature we can no longer merely concern ourselves with conventional notions of linguistic equivalence, or ideas of loss and gain which have long been a consideration in translation theory. For these texts written by postcolonial bilingual subjects create a language "in between" and therefore come to occupy a space "in between." In most cases, the challenge of such space "in between" has been double: these texts seek to decolonize themselves from two oppressors at once, namely the western ex-colonizer who naively boasts of their existence and ultimately recuperates them and the "traditional," "national," cultures which shortsightedly deny their importance and conse-quently marginalize them.' Samia Mehrez, 'Translation and the Postcolonial Experience: The Francophone North African Text,' in Lawrence Venuti (ed.), *Rethinking Translation. Discourse, Subjectivity, Ideology*, p. 121.
8. Cf. Edward Said, *Orientalism* (London: Penguin, 1991 [1978]), pp. 66–68.
9. Cf. Richard Jacquemond, 'Translation and Cultural Hegemony: The Case of French-Arabic Translation,' in Lawrence Venuti (ed.), *Rethinking Translation: Discourse, Subjectivity, Ideology*, p. 150.
10. Talal Asad, 'The Concept of Cultural Translation,' in James Clifford and George E. Marcus (eds), *Writing Culture. The Poetics and Politics of Ethnography* (Berkeley: University of California Press, 1986), p. 148.
11. Cf. Samia Mehrez, 'Translation and the Postcolonial Experience: The Francophone North African Text', in Lawrence Venuti (ed.), *Rethinking Translation. Discourse, Subjectivity, Ideology*, p. 121.
12. *Ibid.*, p. 122.

13. Talal Asad, 'The Meaning of Translation,' in *Writing Culture*, p. 162.
14. Italo Calvino, *Si una noche de invierno un viajero* . . . (Madrid: Siruela, 1989), pp. 143–144 (our translation).
15. Venuti, 'Introduction,' *Rethinking Translation*, p. 5.
16. Cf. M. Carmen África Vidal, 'Traducir por la izquierda', *Ensayos sobre traducción*, Ramón López Ortega, ed. (Cáceres: Universidad de Extremadura, 1994).
17. Cf. André Lefevere, *Translation, Rewriting, and the Manipulation of Literary Fame* (London and New York: Routledge, 1992), pp. 1–10.
18. Robert Scholes, *Textual Power* (New Haven and London: Yale University Press, 1985), p. 15.
19. André Lefevere, 'Holy Garbage, tho' by Homer cook't', *Traduction, terminologie, redaction* 1, 2 (1988), p. 26.
20. Talal Asad, 'The Concept of Cultural Translation in British Social Anthropology,' in James Clifford and George E. Marcus (eds), *Writing Culture: The Poetics and Politics of Ethnography*, p. 163.

2 The Meek or the Mighty: Reappraising the Role of the Translator

SUSAN BASSNETT

There is a long-standing, deep-rooted impulse on the part of translators and translation specialists to evangelicize, to preach the gospel which proclaims that despite the lowliness of our estate, the work we do is nevertheless significant. Translation, as we never tire of reminding people, is all too often poorly paid, it is work that demands a high degree of skill but is repaid with low status and low regard. Someone who may have spent a lifetime translating can still be dismissed as 'just a translator', and where a translator may have acquired a reputation for other kinds of writings also, one often finds editors classifying translations in a sub-category along with juvenilia or early drafts. Translation has been frequently contrasted unfavourably with 'original' writing, as a kind of lesser activity, or as a form of training for the 'real' business of writing. In an essay entitled 'Confessions of a Translator', Ralph Nelson muses on the problem of distinguishing between writing and translating:

> I was too young in the crime of art to ask myself: Is it healthy for a poet to translate? Is it true that translating is next to Poetry-ness, a good piece of work while waiting for the Visitation?[1]

This question has preoccupied writers/translators for a very long time. The Earl of Roscommon (1633–85) struggles with the distinction between the two types of writing and comes to an important conclusion:

> 'Tis true, Composing is the nobler Part,
> But good Translation is no Easie Art,
> For the materials have long since been found,
> Yet both your Fancy and your Hands are bound,
> And by improving what was writ before,
> Invention labours less, but Judgement more.

Each poet with a different talent writes,
One praises, one instructs, another bites.
Horace did ne'er aspire to Epick Bays,
Nor lofty Maro stoop to Lyrick Lays.
Examine how your Humour is inclin'd,
And which the Ruling Passion of your Mind;
Then seek a Poet who your ways does bend,
And choose an Author as you choose a Friend;
United by this sympathetick Bond,
You grow familiar, intimate and fond.
Your Thoughts, your Words, your Stiles, your Souls agree,
No longer his Interpreter, but He.[2]

This famous passage recognizes a distinction between the act of translating and the act of creating a completely new piece of writing, but defends translation in strong terms. True, the greatest praise goes to composition, but the skills involved in the translation process are special ones. Roscommon acknowledges that the task of the translator is to improve on the source text, and suggests that the faculty which comes most into play here is judgement rather than invention. Having defended the translator in principle, he goes on to point out the variety of writing and offers advice to anyone interested in translating. The translator is to choose carefully, to select an author with whom there is a sense of empathy, what he terms 'a sympathetick bond'. Through this relationship and by means of a close reading of the source author's work, a symbiosis takes place and the translator and author of the source text are fused in a mystical orgasmic relationship where they cease to exist as separate entities and become one. The last line says it all: the translator ceases to be an interpreter and becomes the source writer for the target reader.

This view of the author-translator relationship bears strong similarities to post-modernist theories of the writer-reader-translator relationship. Recent translation theory has stressed the vital role of the translator in the interpretive process, and has moved away from the old idea of the translator as a betrayer of the pure source text. Derrida argues that translation serves to remind us that there is no absolute meaning, no uncontested original. The act of translating is dynamic, bringing texts together in a play of multiple meanings:

Difference is never pure, no more so is translation, and for the notion of translation we would have to substitute a notion of *transformation*: a regulated transformation of one language by another, of one text by another. We will never have, and in fact never had, to do with some 'transport' of pure signifieds from one language to another, or within one and the same language, that the signifying instrument would leave virgin and untouched.[3]

Derrida's approach to translation has much in common with the Earl of Roscommon's views, for both draw attention to the process of exchange and interchange that takes place during translating, and both use the metaphoric language of human relationships to illustrate their argument. Roscommon depicts the translator gradually becoming so involved with the source author that a mysterious transformation takes place and the two are fused into a new oneness. Derrida draws upon the figurative language of Walter Benjamin, and the distinction between *überleben* (to survive) and *fortleben* (to sur-vive, to continue living) to show how the translation ensures the continuity of the source text, in direct contrast to the old notion of the translation as diminution of the source, or a betrayal of it. Translation therefore becomes the act that ensures the life of the text and guarantees its survival. Far from traducing the pure original, the translation injects new life blood into a text by bringing it to the attention of a new world of readers in a different language. Octavio Paz celebrates translation as a means of helping us to understand the multi-faceted world we live in:

> On the one hand, the world is presented to us as a collection of similarities; on the other, as a growing heap of texts, each slightly different from the one that came before it: translations of translations of translations. Each text is unique, yet at the same time it is the translation of another text. No text can be completely original because language itself, in its very essence, is already a translation – first from the nonverbal world, and then, because each sign and each phrase is a translation of another sign, another phrase.[4]

This positive, assertive perspective on translation is a welcome change after a long period during which translation has been seen in a more negative light. The discourse of translation has tended to stress that negativity; translation has been described as 'secondary', 'mechanical', 'derivative', a translation is a 'copy', a 'substitute', a poor version of the superior original. This discourse dooms the translator from the outset, for the enterprise of translating is thus viewed as less valuable than other forms of writing. Translation in this paradigm is a servile activity and the translated text stands in a lower position *vis-à-vis* the hegemonic position of the source text.

Resistance to the notion of translation as a secondary, second class activity has accelerated in recent years, parallel to the development of the discipline of Translation Studies and to the theoretical work that has reconsidered the power relationship between writer and reader. The notion of the death of the author must inevitably lead to the death of the original, and once the original ceases to be, the translation can no longer be perceived as subsidiary to it and the translator is released from thrall to the all-powerful source.

The development of polysystems theory in the 1970s changed the nature of translation analysis and led to the great expansion in the field that has come to be known as Translation Studies. Central to the polysystems approach were certain key assumptions about translation, most crucial of which was the recognition of the role played by translation in shaping the literary polysystem. Far from being considered a marginal activity, translation was perceived as having played a fundamental part in literary and cultural history. Translation could be documented as having been at various moments subversive, innovatory or radical. A good example of the subversive power of translation is the case of the translation of the Bible into vernacular languages in the Middle Ages, where the penalty for heretical interpretations of the sacred text was death. The innovatory power of translation is testified to on countless occasions when new forms, new material, and new ideas were introduced across cultural frontiers through the efforts of translators. A case of translation being a radical form of social protest is reflected in the surge of translation activity during the struggles to assert the national identities of many states in central and southern Europe in the early nineteenth century. Byron, in the preface to his *Prophecy of Dante* (defined by him an imitation, not a translation) notes that 'the Italians are particularly jealous of all that is left to them as a nation – their literature'[5] thereby showing that he had understood the relationship between language and identity that shaped the nationalist thinking of his time. By refusing to translate from the Italian, Byron was effectively declaring his solidarity with the Italian independence cause, and agreeing that if a literature belongs to a nation, then in certain circumstances translation can be perceived as theft, as a violation of the right of a language to keep its own literature to itself.

The combination of the new historiography introduced by the polysystems theorists and their successors, combined with a re-evaluation of the authority of the source text has finally broken the stranglehold in which translation has been held for more than two centuries. We are now in a position to consider the diachronics of translating in European languages and to question the starting point of the discourse of negativity and subsidiarity that has so dominated the discussion of translation and so affected the status of translators themselves.

It is generally considered that Etienne Dolet's (1509–46) *La manière de bien traduire d'une langue en aultre* (The way to translate well from one language to another) is the earliest treatise on translation in a modern European language. Printed in 1540, it lays down five basic rules for the translator to follow. Firstly, the translator must 'understand perfectly the meaning and the subject matter of the author he translates'[6]. This is to ensure that the translator may avoid obscurity and produce a translation that is clear and intelligible. Secondly, the translator must have perfect knowledge of the source language and have 'achieved the same excellence in the language he wants to translate into'. This is to ensure that neither language is in any way diminished, and is quite a radical view of translation, for it insists particularly on the need for expertise in the source language. Thirdly, and significantly, the translator must 'not enter into slavery' by translating word for word. This metaphor reinforces Dolet's assertion that the role of the translator is an active one, and that the relationship between writer and translator is one of equality and not of subservience. This leads him on to his fourth point, which concerns the development of vernacular languages, a crucially important issue in Renaissance Humanist Europe. What Dolet proposes is for the translator to be bold enough to use the language of common currency and to avoid archaisms or excessive latinisms. The translator should avoid 'novelties spawned by curiosity' and should use rare words only in cases of dire need. Finally, the translator should 'observe the figures of speech' and arrange words 'with such sweetness that the soul is satisfied and the ears are pleased'. The need for the translator to create a text that is harmonious and pleasing to the reader is, says Dolet, absolutely fundamental. Without observation of this rule, all translations will be 'heavy and unpleasant'.

Six years after the publication of the five rules for good translation, which were to have formed part of a larger project on the art of poetry, Dolet was hanged and burned at the stake. His accusers condemned him to death for heresy, on account of his translation not of a Christian text, but of a text by Plato. Theo Hermans suggests that the seeds of Dolet's distraction were already visible in the five rules, for Dolet was advocating not only a set of practical guidelines for translators but also a radical cultural policy[7]. By emphasizing the need for stylistic harmony and for the use of a common language, Dolet was asserting the right of modern languages to the same status as that enjoyed by the ancient languages. Despite the prevailing belief of ecclesiastical authorities in the supremacy of the Latin or Greek 'originals', Dolet argued that vernacular languages could carry equal weight. What he was effectively proposing with the five rules was therefore a notion of translation as a vital element in the creation of a national culture.

Dolet's English humanist counterpart, Sir Thomas More (1477–1535), was equally aware of the power of translation as a shaping force in culture. In his polemic against the Bible translator William Tyndale (c.1494–1536), who was also burned at the stake in Antwerp for heretical translation activities, More shows how the subtle use of language could alter the interpretation of the Scriptures:

> He changed the word church into this word congregation, because he would bring it in question which were the church and set forth Luther's heresy that the church which we should all believe and obey, is not the common known body of all Christian realms remaining in the faith of Christ . . . and he changed priest into senior because he intended to set forth Luther's heresy teaching that priesthood is no sacrament but the office of a lay man or a lay woman appointed by the people to preach. And he changed penance into repenting because he would set forth Luther's heresy teaching that penance is no sacrament.[8]

More's attack on Tyndale exposes the ideological implications of translation practice. Lefevere argues that a culture scrutinizes translation with special attention wherever the text being translated is perceived as central to that culture.[9] Hence the Bible, especially in the period of the Reformation, came under particular scrutiny, and translators suspected of deviating from the accepted normative meaning were severely punished. For More, the use of the vernacular by Tyndale offered a means of making doctrinal changes to the Bible by subtle use of the language, and this he found an unacceptable heresy. Tyndale, for his part, could have claimed that he was merely following Dolet's advice to good translators, and seeking satisfaction with common usage. Nevertheless, there was a fine line between 'englishing' the Bible and rewriting it from a reformist position, and it was the assessment of where a translator stood on that line that meant the difference between life and death. Martin Luther, of course, distinguished between *übersetzen* and *verdeutschen*, and in Northern Europe the question of linguistic and cultural politics was intimately linked to religion.

Dolet's *La manière de bien traduire* . . . was not only the first systematic statement in a vernacular language about translation methodology; it was also a statement that acknowledged the ideological dimension of translation practice, recognizing that far more happens when we translate than merely the transferrence of a text across a language boundary. The French

Inquisition was fully cognizant of that too, hence Dolet's tragic and untimely end.

Dolet proclaimed the freedom of the translator, rejecting the notion of enslavement to the source text. The image of the translator as slave, compelled to obey the source text and its author, developed in the sixteenth and seventeenth centuries, the age of great colonialist expansion outside Europe. Dryden in his dedication to his translation of *The Aeneid* (1697) complained that translators were 'slaves', forced to 'labour on another man's plantation'. This hierarchical model of translation contrasts with the way in which translation was viewed in earlier centuries, and is linked to changes in both the perception and evaluation of cultural products. The invention of printing had given the author a new status as owner or proprietor of the book. The idea of a common pool of material from which authors could draw, as exemplified in a text such as Mallory's late fifteenth century *Morte d'Arthur*, which refers throughout to unspecified French source texts with no sense of subservience or inhibition, was replaced with the concept of the 'original', the text that had a clear point of origin, a clear proprietor and a clearly demarcated frontier. As the notion of the original expanded, so the notion of the translation as a not-original, a sort of derivative or copy also grew.

The changes in perception of translation and original are paralleled by changes in the perception of the colony and its European origins. If we consider the etymology of the term 'colony' in English, which derives from the Latin *colonia*, we find significant shifts of meaning within a very short period. In 1548, two years after Dolet's execution, the term referred simply to a settlement in a new country. By 1550, it was being used to refer to a settlement of people from home, and as an independent self-governed state. By 1612, the usage had shifted so that the meaning encompassed the territory peopled in this way, and by 1711 it had come to be used to describe people of one nationality residing in another place. These subtle changes of meaning reflect changes in social reality and hegemonic change. The initial pattern of the small settlement had expanded and become much more complex in terms of its relations to the point of departure. The gradual development of an idea of an original, something inherently superior to any versions of it, whether textual or colonial, established the starting point as the dominant partner, and meant also that any variation to the source text by the translator could be classified as a betrayal. Significantly, for translation and other forms of textual practice, that dominance was frequently depicted in gender terms.

Feminist scholarship has increasingly questioned the gender bias of the concept of the *belles infidèles*, that acquired such prominence from the seventeenth century onwards. In her lucid essay examining the recurrence of metaphors describing translation that compare it to a sexual act with a dominant (male) partner and a subservient (female) one, Lori Chamberlain shows how the ideal of fidelity on the part of the translator came to be depicted in gendered terms.[10] The translation, like a woman, is bound to be unfaithful if it/she is beautiful. This metaphor has the double effect of both reducing woman to an inferior position *vis-à-vis* her male partner, and reducing translation to an inferior position *vis-à-vis* the source text. We are a very, very long way away from Dolet's idealisation of the free translator expanding language and creating something beautiful and enduring.

But although the image of the translator as slave or as dutiful wife proliferated in the late Renaissance and continued for several centuries, there was also another, seemingly contradictory, perspective on translation and the translator's role. Dryden described himself as a toiler on another man's plantation, but he also boldly declared his independence and stated that:

> A translator that would write with any force or spirit of an original must never dwell on the words of his author. He ought to possess himself entirely and perfectly comprehend the genius and sense of his author, the nature of the subject, and the terms of the art or subject treated of. And then he will express himself as justly and with as much life as if he wrote an original: whereas he who copies word for word loses all the spirit in the tedious transfusion.[11]

The distinction that Dryden is making here is presented in terms of the old word for word vs. sense for sense distinction, but argued in revealing new terms. The translator should 'possess himself' of the author, reversing the slave-master relationship and should effectively become the original. This is the same line of argument proposed by Roscommon, but it is curious to find Dryden seemingly advocating two opposite translation strategies. On the one hand, he depicts the translator as bound in a servile relationship to the source text, whilst on the other hand he urges the translator to go beyond words and possess himself of the source completely.

An explanation of this apparent contradiction may be found in the differing usage of the term 'translation' in the seventeenth century to describe several different textual practices which became confused with one another. These different usages can be unravelled into three distinct strands. Firstly, as the debates on establishing 'rules' for poetic translation show, there was lively concern for the status and rights of the translator.

Dryden, De La Motte, Perrot d'Ablancourt, Cesarotti, Bodmer and many others proposed a range of radical strategies for the translator to follow. De La Motte, for example, abridged Homer, claiming that he had kept those parts of the *Iliad* worth keeping and changing many parts that he felt were unacceptable. The Abbé Prévost (1697–1763) reduced the seven volumes of the English edition of Richardson's *Pamela* to four, explaining that he did so because of the difficulties French readers might have with English customs:

> I have suppressed English customs where they may appear shocking to other nations, or made them conform to customs prevalent in the rest of Europe. It seemed to me that those reminders of the old and uncouth British ways, which only habit prevents the British themselves from noticing, would dishonour a book in which manners should be noble and virtuous.[12]

Criticizing this approach to translation, Johann Jakob Bodmer (1698–1783) contrasts not only French and English taste but also the two nations. He argues that nations are also subject to that which may be observed in classes or individuals, suggesting that a 'rough, warlike nation' and a 'weak, effeminate' one will expose their differences through language:

> Everyone admires the virile, generous nature characteristic of the English nation and expressed in its language. It is easy to see why it has taken so many figurative expressions from blood, death and so on. The English fashion easy-to-use images of things other nations abhor. From childhood on they observe the casual way with which suicide is treated, the general contempt for life, the many fights among men and animals. For this reason an English writer of tragedies is under the obligation, so to speak, of putting the tragic ending of his story (or at least the effects of it) on the stage, before the spectator's eyes, whereas the shocked eyes and the weak hearts of the French would never allow this.[13]

Bodmer's approach is one which takes into account the expectations of the target readership as much as the authority of the source text, and though his generalized assumptions about the spirit or soul of a nation are unacceptably partisan today, his location of translation practice in a wider cultural context established him as a precursor of culturally oriented translation theory. The debates of this period reveal a number of different positions, but throughout the right of the translator to amend the source, improve it, change it, abridge it, etc. are maintained.

Alongside the debates on poetic translation, however, there was another very different idea of translation. This other perspective saw translation as a pedagogical instrument, an intrinsic part of a language-learning process. Translation in the classroom had to be assessed, and hence the notion of faithfulness to the source text was a crucial one. In the age of dictionaries, the bilingual dictionary as a tool for translators posited the idea of equivalence as sameness across linguistic frontiers. Difference was elided in this view of translation; whatever was said in one language could and should be rendered into another, and the success of that rendering was gauged in terms of the faithfulness of the copy to the original. School text books presupposed a binary relationship between languages, with trans-lation as a servile activity designed to show the competence of the student in understanding the source and rendering it into an acceptable version in the target language. The idea that a translator might possess himself of the spirit of the source text was totally unacceptable in the language learning classroom, where norms of fidelity reigned supreme. Yet the term 'translation' was used for both activities.

It was also used for a third type of literary activity, the rendering of a text in one language into another at high speed and for specific commercial purposes. The expansion of mass publishing aimed at the emergent middle classes in the late seventeenth century led to a demand for material to supply the needs of the customers. Likewise, the proliferation of theatres for the new middle classes meant a demand for new plays or for translated plays to fill up a programme. Dryden comments on the role played by booksellers in disseminating translations, recognizing that neither literary merit nor status hold any weight in the world of commerce:

> Booksellers are . . . more devoted to their own gain than the public honour. They are very parsimonious in rewarding the wretched scribblers they employ and care not how the business is done, so that it be but done. They live by selling titles, not books, and if that carry off one impression they have their ends, and value not the curses they and their authors meet with from the bubbled chapmen. While translations are thus at the disposal of the booksellers and have no better judges or rewarders of the performance, it is impossible that we should make any progress.[14]

In this high speed world of mass publishing, the role of translators was simply to supply basic material regardless of quality. The translator as hack writer emerged on the scene, often contrasted negatively with 'real' writers. Sir John Denham was brutally dismissive:

> Such is our pride, our folly and our fate
> That few, but such as cannot write, translate.

Three distinct activities, the poetic, the pedagogical and commercial, all termed as translation were being practiced simultaneously, and their distinct discourses became intertwined. At one end of the scale, the pedagogical insisted upon a rigid normative idea of faithfulness to the original, whilst at the other end the translator could have absolute freedom to do what he or she liked with the original. The difference between the poetic and the commercial, however, is that whilst some translators were primarily concerned with aesthetic effect and took pains to think through their relationship with the source, the pressures placed on translators by the market place meant that the aesthetic was low on a list of priorities. Translators were frequently despised as hacks, and attacked for incompetence, sloppiness and infidelity. Hence the dichotomy that Dryden exposes in his writings on translation: a translator could indeed be a slave and yet a translator could also enjoy a relationship of equality with the source, depending on the terms of reference within which he or she was working.

The confusion about translation that is at its most obvious in the Enlightenment may help to explain the schizophrenic attitude to translation so frequently expressed ever since. In Dolet's time, the power of the translator was recognized as a force that shaped the source text into something other, a force that could be highly subversive. By Dryden's time, that recognition was clouded by the use of translation conceived of as a binary language-learning exercise, in which success was gauged according to the degree of adherence of the target text to the source, and by the pressures imposed upon translation by the market place. If the writer had by now become the owner or proprietor of the original, the translator was relegated to a lesser position, paid accordingly and treated like a servant.

The idea of translation as a lowlier kind of writing persisted for centuries, and to some extent is still with us today. Translators are frequently poorly paid, their work often regarded as inferior, despite the insistence by a huge number of eminent writers throughout the world on the complexity of translation and on its importance. With the development of literary studies at universities in the nineteenth century, the role of translation remained unclarified, the translation occupying an uncomfortable position out on the margins, despite the proliferation of translation practice during the great age of revolutions in Europe and the Americas. The emergence of comparative literature did little to alter this situation, and the study of translation was all too often a subcategory of literary history, if indeed it was studied at all.

As we come to the end of the twentieth century, however, it is clear that this attitude has changed, and for several different reasons. Globally, this is the age of mass communications, of multi-media experiences and a world where audiences demand to share the latest text, be it film, song or book, simultaneously across cultures. Nor has the development of English as a world language slowed down the process of translation; it has, on the contrary, served to emphasize the significance of translation, as questions of cultural politics appear on the agenda. For, as post-colonial theory shows so clearly, language and power are intimately linked. The notion that a translation might be a transparent copy of a superior original is no longer tenable, just as it would not have been tenable in Dolet's time either. Post-colonial translation theorists such as Haraldo de Campos in Brazil, Harish Trivedi in India or Sherry Simon in Canada, to name but three, insist that the study and practice of translation is inevitably an exploration of power relationships within textual practice that reflect power structures within the wider cultural context. Translation, Bassnett and Lefevere maintain:

> like all (re)writings is never innocent. There is always a context in which the translation takes place, always a history from which a text emerges and into which a text is transposed.[15]

Exploring ways in which translation reflects the discourse of colonization, Tejaswini Niranjana argues that translation has traditionally produced strategies of containment. She sees the Enlightenment as the moment when translation came to be used to underwrite practices of subjectification, and contends that only now has the understanding of those processes come to be reconsidered. For Niranjana, this is the moment of a post-colonial analysis of translation practice, that exposes the fallacy of the translator as an unbiased, transparent medium through which a text may pass purportedly along a horizontal axis:

> Translation as a practice shapes, and takes shape within, the asymmetrical relations of power that operate under colonialism . . . In creating coherent and transparent texts and subjects, translation participates – across a range of discourses – in the *fixing* of colonized cultures, making them seem static and unchanging rather than historically constructed. Translation functions as a transparent presentation of something that already exists.[16]

Translation can therefore be seen as reflecting the colonial experience; the source/original holds the power, the colony/copy is disempowered but placated through the myth of transparency and objectivity of the translation. The colony, in short, is perceived as a translation, never as an original, but this is concealed by a promise of equitable textual relations. Hence the current interest on the part of many translation scholars in

post-colonial societies to reconsider the implications of the status of
translation and to posit an alternative to the European Enlightenment view
of the translation process.

In the 1970s, the key word in Translation Studies was 'history'.
Polysystems theory invited reconsideration of the role of translation in
literary history, and startling revisions of accepted knowledge were the
result. That process is still going on, and the history of translation in theory
and in practice is a rich field for scholars. This phase can be compared to
the similar phase in gender studies, when women began the task of
uncovering from history those traces of work by women and men who had
been erased by the mainstream. By the 1980s, with a rethinking of cultural
history and the formation of literary canons well under way, the emphasis
shifted to the question of power relationships between writers, translators
and readers, again parallel to developments in gender studies and in
post-structuralism. The idea of the origin came under scrutiny, and both
Derrida and de Campos, by rereading Benjamin, formulated the concept
of translation that *becomes* the original by virtue of its coming into existence
after the source. Benjamin argues that because it comes later than its source,
and since a text never finds its chosen translator at the time of origin, the
translation marks the continued life of the text at another moment in time.
It is easy to see why this view of translation should have had such impact
on those scholars seeking to re-examine the premises of translation by
deconstructing gender norms and dominant cultural norms. In Benjamin's
reading, translation becomes a liberating act, and the translator becomes
the liberator.

Now, in the 1990s, drawing upon the work of the past two decades, the
keyword is 'visibility'. The role of the translator can be reassessed in terms
of analysing the intervention of the translator in the process of linguistic
transfer. Once considered a subservient, transparent filter through which
a text could and should pass without adulteration, the translation can now
be seen as a process in which that intervention is crucial. Barbara Johnson's
advocation of the need to reread texts that are deemed significant in order
to 'become aware of the repressions, the elisions, the contradictions and the
liguistic slippages that have functioned unnoticed'[17] is also an invitation to
the scholar of translation to look again at the translation process as reflected
in translations themselves, in order to expose contradictions that mirror
the age in which they were made.

There has never been a better time to study translations. From being a
marginal activity outside linguistics proper, at the edges of literary study,
neglected by anthropologists, ethnographers and philosophers, translation

is now being reconsidered, and its fundamental importance in intercultural transfer processes is becoming more apparent. As Andrew Benjamin suggests:

> Within contemporary philosophical work there is a preoccupation, if not a fascination, with translation. It provides the 'concept' in terms of which the possibility, if not the actual practice, of philosophy is discussed. At the same time it also provides a way into an analysis for the transmission of culture.[18]

We have come full circle, back to a recognition of the power invested in the translator to change texts and so change the world. We may not burn translators at the stake (though the attacks on Salman Rushdie's translators show that the translator was certainly not seen as an invisible filter) but we are compelled now to recognize the role they play in reshaping texts, a role that is far from innocent, and is very visible indeed.

Notes

1. Ralph Nelson, 'Confessions of a Translator', *Translation Review* 32/33, 1990.
2. Dillon Wentworth, Earl of Roscommon, 'Essay on Translated Verse', reprinted in André Lefevere (ed.), *Translation/History/Culture: A Sourcebook* (London: Routledge, 1992), pp. 43–5.
3. Jacques Derrida, *Positions*, trans. Alan Bass (Chicago: University of Chicago Press, 1981), p. 20.
4. Octavio Paz, 'Translation: Literature and Letters', trans. Irene del Corral, in Rainer Schulte and John Biguenet (eds), *Theories of Translation. An Anthology of Essays from Dryden to Derrida* (Chicago: University of Chicago Press, 1992), pp. 152–63.
5. George Gordon, Lord Byron, 'Preface' to *The Prophecy of Dante*, 1819.
6. Etienne Dolet, 'La manière de bien traduire d'une langue en aultre', in Lefevere (ed.), *op. cit.*, pp. 27–8.
7. Theo Hermans, unpublished lecture, University of Warwick, Spring 1993.
8. Sir Thomas More, 'Confutation of Tyndale's Answer', in Lefevere, *op. cit.*, pp. 71–2.
9. Lefevere, *op. cit.*, p. 70.
10. Lori Chamberlain, 'Gender and the Metaphorics of Translation', in Lawrence Venuti (ed.), *Rethinking Translation. Discourse, Subjectivity, Ideology* (London: Routledge, 1992), pp. 57–75.
11. John Dryden, 'The Life of Lucian, in George Watson (ed.), *John Dryden: Dramatic Poesy and Other Essays*, vol. II (London: Dent, 1962). Extracts reprinted in Schulte and Biguenet, *op. cit.*
12. Antoine Prévost, 'Preface to his translation of *Pamela*', in Lefevere, *op. cit.*, pp. 39–40.
13. Johann Jakob Bodmer, 'Ninety-fourth Letter in *der Maler der Sitten*', in Lefevere, *op. cit.*, pp. 124–8.
14. Dryden, *op. cit.*

15. Susan Bassnett and André Lefevere (eds), *Translation, History and Culture* (London: Pinter, 1990), p. 11.
16. Tejaswini Niranjana, *Siting Translation. History, Post-Structuralism and the Colonial Text* (Berkeley and Los Angeles: University of California Press, 1992), p. 3.
17. Barbara Johnson, 'The Surprise of Otherness: A Note on the Wartime Writings of Paul de Man', in Peter Collier and Helga Geyer-Ryan (eds), *Literary Theory Today* (Cambridge: Polity Press, 1990).
18. Andrew Benjamin, *Translation and the Nature of Philosophy* (London: Routledge, 1989), p. 9.

3 Norms and the Determination of Translation: A Theoretical Framework

THEO HERMANS

1

Although Translation Studies today constitutes anything but a unified field of study, some of its larger disciplinary shifts have been felt more or less across the entire range of the subject. At an early stage, for example, 'fidelity' was replaced by 'equivalence' as a theoretical and methodological concept in applied as well as in descriptive and theoretical approaches to translation. In the last ten years or so, 'equivalence' too has been progressively questioned and hollowed out, largely in favour of the concept of 'norms'.

Perhaps the first step in the direction of the current preoccupation with norms was taken in Jiři Levý's work, in particular in his essay on 'Translation as a Decision Process',[1] which viewed translation in terms of games theory and the practical reasoning involved in decision-making. The concept itself, however, was introduced into translation studies by Gideon Toury,[2] who deployed it as an operational tool in his descriptive approach. For Toury, translational norms govern the decision-making process in translating, and hence they determine the type of equivalence that obtains between original and translation. He also distinguished different types of norms, and commented on ways of discovering them. In practice, Toury saw norms mostly as constraints on the translator's behaviour,[3] and he gave only a brief indication of the broader, social function of norms.

Since then, the concept has continued to receive attention in Translation Studies.[4] At the same time, the nature and functioning of norms, rules and conventions have been highlighted in a number of publications covering a variety of other disciplines, from law and linguistics to ethics and international relations.[5] The recent collection *Rules and Conventions*, edited by Mette Hjort,[6] ranges from philosophy and literature to social theory; in her introduction Hjort stresses precisely the interdisciplinary relevance and applicability of rules and conventions.[7] Given the nature of translation and of Translation Studies, an approach through these concepts may well be productive, especially if we wish to focus on the social dimension of translating and on the place of translation in relation to power and ideology.

Norms are psychological and social entities. They constitute an important factor in the interaction between people, and as such are part of every socialization process. In essence, norms, like rules and conventions (I will distinguish later), have a socially regulatory function. They help to bring about the coordination required for continued coexistence with other people. In doing so norms 'safeguard the conditions of social coexistence',[8] for they usefully mediate between the individual and the collective sphere, between an individual's intentions, choices and actions, and collectively held beliefs, values and preferences. Moreover, norms and conventions contribute to the stability of interpersonal relations, and hence of groups, communities and societies, by reducing contingency, unpredictability, and the uncertainty which springs from our inability to control time or to predict the actions of fellow human beings. The reduction of contingency brought about by norms and conventions is a matter of generalizing from past experience and of making reasonably reliable, more or less prescriptive projections concerning similar types of situations in the future.

2

Translation used to be regarded primarily in terms of relations between texts, or between language systems. Today it is increasingly seen as a complex transaction taking place in a communicative, socio-cultural context. This requires that we bring the translator as a social being fully into the picture.

Translation involves a network of active social agents, who may be individuals or groups, each with certain preconceptions and interests. The translative operation is a matter of transactions between parties that have an interest in these transactions taking place. For those involved in the transfer, the various modalities and procedures that go with it presuppose choices, alternatives, decisions, strategies, aims and goals. Norms play a crucial role in these processes. In what follows the emphasis will be on the agents involved in these processes rather than on the nature of the relation between source and target texts. I will refer to norms primarily as social and cultural realities, rather in the way that sociologists or anthropologists might use the term.

It is worth pointing out at the start that, as regards translation, norms are relevant to the entire transfer operation, not just the actual process of translating, if only because this latter process is necessarily preceded by a number of other decisions. Translation may be regarded as a particular mode of discursive transfer between cultural circuits or systems. It constitutes one among a number of possible modes of the intercultural movement of texts. Other modes include, for example, importing or exporting a text in untranslated form – although it might be noted that deploying materially the same text in a different linguistic and cultural environment will still lend that text a different 'load', for it is bound to be perceived differently; Anthony Pym rightly speaks of 'value transformation'[9] in such cases of physical transfer. Summary, paraphrase, gloss, critical commentary and other forms of what André Lefevere broadly calls 'rewriting'[10] constitute a further set of alternative modes, as do transformations into other semiotic media, and so on.

The choice of one or other mode of transfer is initially made by whoever is the prime mover instigating the process. This may be an agent in the source culture or, more usually, in the target culture. The initial choice may be delegated, and it may turn out to be impracticable. Whether the choice of a particular mode of transfer is practicable in a given situation, is largely determined by the situation and by the 'rules of the game' at that moment. The initial choice of a preferred or intended mode of import may be modified by the initiator's assessment of what is materially possible in terms of various physical factors (technology, geography, etc.), and of what is socially, politically, culturally and/or ideologically feasible, i.e. what is likely to be tolerated, permitted, encouraged or demanded by those who control the means of production and distribution and by the relevant institutions and channels in economic, social, ideological and artistic terms.

Intercultural traffic, then, of whatever kind, takes place in a given social context, a context of complex structures, including power structures. It involves agents who are both conditioned by these power structures or at least entangled in them, and who exploit or attempt to exploit them to serve their own ends and interests, whether individual or collective. The power structures cover political and economic power but also, in the field of cultural production, those forms which Pierre Bourdieu calls 'symbolic power'. The agents, faced with an array of possible options, have to make choices and decisions about how to proceed.

It is here that the concept of norms can be usefully brought in. They facilitate and guide the process of decision-making. Norms govern the mode of import of cultural products – for example, of the translation of literary texts – to a considerable extent, at virtually every stage and every level, whenever choices between alternative courses of action need to be made (to import or not to import? to translate or to 'rewrite' in some other way? how to translate?). Of course, norms also govern the mode of export, if a culture, or a section of it, actively exports texts or other cultural goods. But whether a product will be *im*ported by the intended receptor system, or imported in the way envisaged by the donor, depends partly on factors pertaining to the receptor system itself and partly on the nature of the relations between the two systems in question.

In practice, this means that norms play a significant part, firstly, in the decision by the relevant agent in the receptor system whether or not to import a foreign-language text, or allow it to be imported; secondly, if it is decided to import, whether to translate (whatever the term may mean in a given socio-cultural configuration) or to opt for some other mode of importation; and thirdly, if it is decided to translate, how to approach the task, and how to see it through.

This latter process is, of course, the translation process itself. I am not interested here in the mental reality – the 'black box' – of the translation process as such or in ways of reconstructing or representing it by means of diagrams and such like. I take it for granted, however, that translating requires constant decision-making by the translator on a number of levels, and over a period of time, since texts are made up of discrete units. This process of decision-making is in large measure, necessarily and benefi- cially, governed by norms. If it were not, translators faced with a source text, however short or simple, would either be unable to opt for one solution rather than another and throw up their hands in despair, or make entirely random decisions, like a computer gone haywire.

From the point of view of the study of translation it is important to bear in mind that this process of decision-making, and hence the operation of norms in it, takes place in the translator's head and thus remains largely hidden from view. We have no direct access to it. We can speculate about it, and we can try to move closer to it through procedures like talk-aloud protocols, or through confronting the input of the process with its output, i.e. the source text with the target text, and then make retrospective inferences. In this latter course we are helped by the fact that translation, like any other use of language, is a communicative act. This means that it constitutes a more or less interactive form of social behaviour, involving a degree of 'interpersonal coordination' among those taking part (selecting and attuning an appropriate code, recognizing and interpreting the code, paying attention, eliminating 'noise', etc.). However, it depends for its success not only on solving the specific 'coordination problems' presented by the immediate situation, but also on the relative positions and qualities of the participants, and on the values and interests at stake. Since these involve issues of material and symbolic power, success too may have to be judged in terms of the interests of one party rather than the other being served. Once we have recognized this social dimension of the production and reception of translations, as distinct from the psychological reality of the translation process, we are in a position to appreciate the role of norms and models, as social realities, in these processes.

3

What exactly is this role?[11] My basic assumption is that translation, like any other use of language, is a communicative act. As was pointed out in the previous paragraph, communication constitutes a form of social behaviour and requires a degree of interpersonal coordination among the agents involved. It follows from this that communication problems can in principle be described in terms of so-called 'interpersonal coordination problems', which in turn are a subset of social interaction problems. Norms, like conventions, offer solutions to problems of this kind. It is this perspective which allows us to apply, or at least to transpose, what social scientists and anthropologists have to say about social conventions, norms, rules and models to the domain of language use and of translation, including the practice of translation as it takes place in a given historical context. In what follows a general term like 'behaviour' comprises such activities as 'speaking', 'writing' and 'translating'.

This aspect of norms can be explained more fully by drawing first on the notion of convention, seen here also in general terms as a social phenomenon with a regulatory function. In his highly influential *Convention: A Philosophical Study*, David Lewis gave a technical definition of convention which might be paraphrased as follows: conventions are regularities in behaviour which have emerged as arbitrary but effective solutions to recurrent problems of interpersonal coordination. Because they have proved effective, these solutions become the preferred course of action for individuals in a given type of situation. Conventions grow out of precedent and social habit, and they presuppose common knowledge and acceptance.

More precisely, they imply a set of mutual expectations: the expectation of others that, in a given situation, I will very probably adopt a certain course of action, and my expectation that others expect me to do just that. Conventions therefore are a matter of social expectations and of 'expectations of expectations', i.e. of reciprocal expectations, or, in Ullmann-Margalit's words, of 'convergent mutual expectations'.[12]

Conventions, in this sense, are not norms, or they are implicit norms at best.[13] They depend on regularities and shared preferences, i.e. on interpersonal coordination within a given community. To the extent, however, that conventions imply acceptance, and the mutual recognition of acceptance, of 'approximately the same preferences regarding all possible combinations of actions',[14] they usefully restrict the number of practically available options in recurrent situations of a given type, and thus make behaviour more predictable by reducing uncertainty and contingency.[15] Although conventions do not presuppose explicit agreements between individuals, they still act as generally accepted social constraints on behaviour.

Over time, conventions may fall victim to their own success. If a convention has served its purpose of solving a recurrent coordination problem sufficiently well for long enough, the expectation, on all sides, that a certain course of action will be adopted in a certain type of situation may grow beyond a mere preference, i.e. beyond a preferential and probabilistic expectation, and acquire a binding character. At that point we can begin to speak of norms.

Norms, then, can be understood as stronger, more prescriptive versions of social conventions. Whereas conventions are a matter of precedent and shared expectation, norms have a directive character. Like conventions, norms derive their legitimacy from shared knowledge, a pattern of mutual expectation and acceptance, and the fact that, on the individual level, they are largely internalized. This is what allows us to speak of norms as both psychological and social entities. There are many social, moral and artistic norms and conventions that we constantly observe while hardly being aware of them.

Norms are prescriptive rules: they have a normative semantic load and are used to guide, control, or change the behaviour of agents with decision-making capacities.[16] Norms differ from conventions in that they tell individual members of a community not just how everyone else *expects* them to behave in a given situation, but how they *ought* to behave. In other words, they imply that there is, among the array of possible options, a particular course of action which is more or less strongly preferred because the community has agreed to accept it as 'proper' or 'correct' or 'appropri-ate'. This is the course of action which therefore *should* be adopted. The intersubjective sense of what is 'correct' constitutes the *content* of a norm. More about this below. First a few more words about the operative aspect of norms, their executive arm, as it were.

Since norms imply a degree of social and psychological pressure, they act as practical constraints on the individual's behaviour by foreclosing certain options and choices, which however always remain available in principle. At the same time, and more positively, they single out and suggest, or prescribe more or less emphatically, a particular selection from among the range of possible courses of action. Ultimately, the directive or normative force of a norm stems either from some kind of social pressure, be it in the form of inducements and rewards or of the threat of sanctions, or from the consenting attitude of the individual addressed by the norm; or indeed from a combination of the two.[17] Strong norms are strongly felt to be appropriate, or backed up by strong sanctions, often spelled out explicitly. But since all action within the scope of conventions and norms requires the individual's consent to some degree, such action is always a form of cooperative action.

To the extent that norms grow out of conventions more or less spontaneously, they derive their legitimacy from the same patterns of mutual expectation characteristic of conventions, and they presuppose a similar degree of social acceptance and internalization on the individual's part. Where norms most resemble conventions they are also at their most permissive. In any case, non-compliance with a norm does not usually result in drastic sanctions for the individual concerned, just as non-compli-ance with a norm in particular instances does not invalidate the norm. Provided the breaches do not occur persistently and on a large scale without any effective sanction, norms are able to cope with a relatively large amount of discrepant behaviour. It is in this sense that Niklas Luhmann speaks of norms as 'counterfactually stabilised behavioural expectations'.[18] The conventions and norms of polite conversation at a dinner party, for example, are not invalidated because one of the guests fails or refuses to observe them. The same goes for, say, the highway code, which is a much stronger and more explicit norm (or rule, see below). In other words, norms can be broken. They do not preclude erratic or idiosyncratic behaviour. Which norms are broken by whom will depend on the nature and strength of the norm and on the individual's motivation.

As the prescriptive force of norms increases from the permissive to the mandatory, from the preferred to the obligatory, they move away from conventions in relying less on mutual expectations and internalized acceptance, and more on rules and instructions, which are often formulated explicitly, i.e. codified and expressed as commands and commandments. The term 'rule' is used here as meaning a strong norm, which in many cases will have become institutionalized. When the pressure exerted by a rule becomes the *only* reason for behaving in one way rather than another, we can speak of decrees. In contrast to conventions, which are non-statutory and impersonal and do not carry institutionalized sanctions, decrees are statutory, and they are issued by an identifiable authority, which has the power to impose sanctions for non-compliance. Here we recognize the hierarchical structure of most social and socio-cultural systems, and the overarching relations of power and authority prevailing within them. Of course, power relations are inscribed in the entire network of norms and conventions operative in societies and their socio-cultural systems; in the case of decrees they manifest themselves in their most naked form. Compared with conventions, therefore, decrees represent the opposite end of the normative scale: they spell out explicit orders, which may be codified positively or negatively, as obligations or as prohibitions.

Broadly speaking, then, norms and rules cover the entire range between conventions and decrees. This range could be set out in a continuum, as follows:

convention – norm – rule – decree

Conventions arise out of precedent and rely on shared habits and mutual expectations which are common knowledge. Norms differ from conventions in that they have a binding character, carry some form of sanction, and may either grow out of customs or be issued by an authorizing instance. Rules are strong norms, usually institutionalized and posited by an identifiable authority, with or without the full assent of the individual subjected to them. Decrees are specific directives issued as commands by a particular authority and backed up by drastic sanctions.[19]

4

Norms and rules, then, can be strong or weak. They may cover a narrow or a broad domain. They may or may not be explicitly posited. They may be positive or negative, i.e. tending towards obligations or towards prohibitions. The 'modalities of normative force', which indicate the relative strength of a norm, together with its positive or negative load, could be mapped diagrammatically in the form of a semiotic square,[20] so that the interrelations between its various modes of operative force become clear (see Figure 3.1).

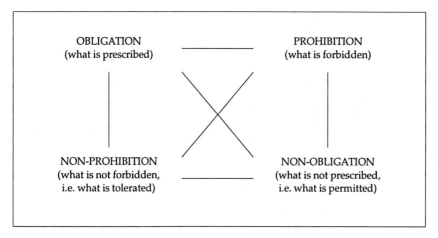

Figure 3.1 Modalities of normative force

Each of these four positions (obligation, negative obligation or prohibition, non-obligation, and non-prohibition) can be written out more fully. This is shown in Figure 3.2, in which A = agent, C = course of action, and neg = negative.

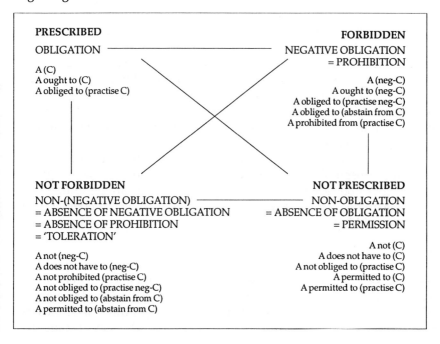

Figure 3.2 Modalities of normative force – 2

In both cases the upper half of the square contains strong, clearly recognized and well-defined norms and rules, formulated as obligations and prohibitions, which may be backed up by sanctions or supported by strong attitudes and belief systems. The lower half indicates areas of permissiveness and of tolerated behaviour: that which one is not obliged to do or say and which therefore 'may' be done or said, and that which one is not obliged to refrain from doing or saying and which therefore 'can' be done or said. On the whole, more permissive norms are also more malleable and hence more open to re-interpretation and adjustment in response to changing circumstances, whereas stronger and more general norms tend to stabilize over time and become institutionalized and 'entrenched', so that they may even be felt to apply in cases where their original justification or rationale no longer holds.[21]

Since norms, as indicated above, may grow out of repeated occurrences falling into a pattern, they apply in a general manner to types of situations, i.e. they involve a degree of generalization and abstraction. When a new situation arises, an individual agent may have to make an interpretive judgement in deciding whether it falls within the scope of one norm rather than another. Indeed there may be more than one possibility, and the agent may have a reason, or an ulterior motive, for referring to one norm rather than another, for example in deciding to translate a text as an historical document rather than as a piece of literature. More stable and entrenched norms and rules usually involve a larger degree of internalization and are more likely to be applied as a matter of course. Either way, the very act of observing a norm confirms and reinforces its validity and scope. This practical aspect is important, since the linguistic formulation of a norm, whether within the community in question or by an outside observer, is different from its directive force in effectively guiding actions in particular situations. In practice, following a given set of norms may be a matter of disposition, of acquired habit, indeed of 'habitus' in Bourdieu's sense of a 'durable, transposable disposition', as Charles Taylor[22] has also argued. Such dispositions are not inherited but inculcated. Learning to translate means learning to operate the norms of translation, i.e. to operate with them and within them.

5

As suggested earlier, the operation of norms implies interaction between agents, and therefore a social context. If in a given field F, and in a given situation, agent A has an obligation to act in a certain way, this means he or she has this obligation towards another agent B, who may of course be a group of persons, a collective, a community. If *A* has an obligation towards *B*, it follows that *B* has a certain claim on *A*. This 'claim' means that *B* has the power to impose a norm on *A* and invoke sanctions in case of non-compliance by *A*, if *B* chooses to use that power.[23] As in the case of the modalities of normative force, the modalities of normative control involve not only a set of clearly defined relations in which *B* controls *A* (expressed below as *B* > *A*), so that *A* has certain, mutually recognized obligations towards *B* to behave in a certain manner on certain occasions, but also a more uncertain area, where *A* is more or less immune from *B* and vice versa. In Figure 3.3 it is again the top half of the diagram which shows clearly defined relations, while the bottom half shows areas of diffuseness and uncertainty.

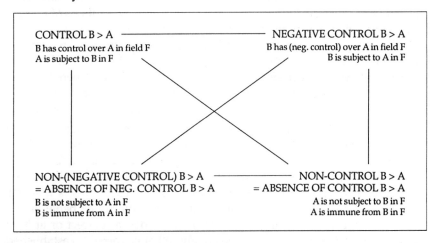

CONTROL B > A ———————— NEGATIVE CONTROL B > A
B has control over A in field F   B has (neg. control) over A in field F
A is subject to B in F   B is subject to A in F

NON-(NEGATIVE CONTROL) B > A ——————— NON-CONTROL B > A
= ABSENCE OF NEG. CONTROL B > A   = ABSENCE OF CONTROL B > A
B is not subject to A in F   A is not subject to B in F
B is immune from A in F   A is immune from B in F

Figure 3.3 Modalities of normative control

A legal contract is more binding than a voluntary code of conduct or a gentlemen's agreement. An experienced and well-established poetry translator may feel more confident than the young aspiring novice in ignoring the wishes and suggestions of a particular editor or publisher. The point to stress, however, is that norms and rules are social realities, involving not just individuals, groups and communities but also the power relations within these communities, whether these relations are material (economic, legal, political) or 'symbolic'. This is what gives the model its dynamic character. Norms operate in a complex and dynamic social context, which may be a cultural domain, such as the domain of literature. It does not greatly matter whether one thinks of this context in terms of a 'system' in the sense of systems theory or in terms of, say, a 'field', such as the field of cultural production in Bourdieu's sense. What is important is the fact that norms are deeply implicated in the social and cultural life of a community. They involve different and often competing positions and possibilities, they point up various interests and stakes being pursued, defended, coveted, claimed – and the individual's desires and strategies to further his or her own ends, whether as a result of rational choices and practical reasoning or of decisions grounded in entrenched norms and rules. In large, complexly structured and stratified societies, a multiplicity of different, overlapping and often conflicting norms coexist. This multiplicity is at the same time the main repository of the potential for change.

It is also the stratified social context, and the hierarchy of the power relations in it, which explains the greater prominence as well as the greater binding force of some norms as opposed to others. The institutions or agents who exercise normative control tend to occupy positions of relative power and dominance in the particular field where the norms apply, or indeed in higher-level fields, i.e. fields closer to the centres of power in a community. Generally speaking the possibility of effectively subverting norms only arises in conditions of weak normative control, when the norm subject is relatively immune to sanctions, or prepared to accept them.

The dominant norms of a community are usually those of the dominant sections of the community. They are also the sections which determine the content of the norms. In themselves, norms are neither true nor false. They do not represent assertions about existing states of affairs. Rather, they stipulate what 'ought' or 'is to' happen, how things 'should' be. The content of a norm is a notion of what is 'proper' or 'correct'. This is a social, intersubjective notion, a conceptualization of patterns of behaviour – including speaking, writing, translating – regarded as correct or at least legitimate, and therefore valued positively. What is 'correct' is established within the community, and within the community's power structures and ideology, and mediated to its members. The directive force of norms, their executive arm, serves among other things to delimit and secure these notions of correctness. The notion of what constitutes 'correct' behaviour, or 'correct' linguistic usage, or 'correct' translation, is a social and cultural construct.

Notions of correctness are abstract entities. They are values, which, in order to become socially or culturally operative, have to be fixed, both subjectively and intersubjectively, so that collective attitudes can be attuned to them. They also have to be learned, and they are constantly reproduced as part of the learning process. In practice, they often appear in the more schematic but mentally manageable form of models, understood here as patterns (e.g. the elements and precepts of a poetics) derived from more abstract prototypical values and instances, or as specific products (e.g. individual texts) recognized as embodying those values. The canonized models are likely to be the models adopted and promoted by the dominant groups in a given community. In that sense we can say that the operation of social and cultural systems is governed by norms and models.

The mere fact of entering a cultural system and learning to operate as a participant in it, involves a process of familiarization with the relevant models. This is true whether we are speaking, say, of going to university, or of joining a translation agency, or of aspiring writers trying to get their poems or literary translations accepted by a publisher. In fact, the process itself has directive and motivational force, as cultural models are internalized, and behaviour is adapted to conform to the models recognized as pertinent to the system.[24] It remains possible, of course, to resist the process of adaptation, but at the cost of a failure to integrate into the system. Looking at it from a different angle, we can say that it is through the motivational force of models and norms that relations of obligation and claim are created between collectives and individuals. These relations are also relations of power.

6

If every stage in the transfer and translation of texts is governed by choices which require criteria to make more than wholly random decisions about which options to select, and to what end, then norms, rules and models supply these criteria and goals. Compliance with the set of translational norms regarded as pertinent in a given community or domain means that the product, i.e. the translation, is likely to conform to the relevant correctness notion, which means conformity with the model embodying that correctness notion – behind which we can discern the dominant values and attitudes of the community or the domain in question. Translating 'correctly', in other words, amounts to translating according to the prevailing norm, and hence in accordance with the relevant, canonized models. The result can be expected to be another 'model' translation.

Learning to translate correctly means the acquisition of the relevant competence, i.e. the set of dispositions required to select and apply those norms and rules that will produce legitimate translations, i.e. translations which conform to the legitimate models.[25] In this way the translator training institute, or any other type of instruction performing the same function, continually reproduces the dominant norms and models, ensuring their canonization and entrenchment. The higher-level authority – a political entity, a economic class, a community – which attaches value to those norms and models, delegates its norm-setting power to the educational institute.

It will be clear that in the case of translating, as a form of textual production, the models being referred to are textual, discursive entities. They cover the substance of what is normally called a 'poetics' (including a 'poetics of translation'), i.e. a set of principles and practical rules for 'good writing', and a set of examples of good practice. But they appear here with a different emphasis, which allows us to appreciate more clearly their strategic role in the dynamics of culture. Particular groups or subgroups may adopt a certain configuration of translational models and prototypes in opposition to other groups, to compete with them and because there are certain material and symbolic stakes to be defended or claimed. As individuals weave their way through and around these configurations, they take up positions and build alliances, so as to be able to achieve their own aims, goals and ambitions as well as those of the groups with which they have aligned themselves. The marked intertextuality which results from these strategies has a social relevance. In translating detective novels or popular romances, for example, the choice of a particular textual model may well mark the translation as 'literary' but it may also spell the end of a lucrative contract. At the same time, the textual models in question are not only, and not necessarily, those of the receptor cuture. The specificity of translation stems from the fact that it refers, expressly or tacitly, to an anterior discourse in another sign system which it claims to represent in one way or another. This not only complicates the intertextual nature of the translated text, which always reaches beyond systemic borders, but it also emphasizes its hybridity, as the systemic 'otherness' of the source is unlikely to be wiped out altogether in translation. Translated texts, we can say, always signal to textual models of at least two cultures.

This context also helps us to appreciate the relative power which the translator has in principle, and may in certain circumstances be able to exploit. Translators normally cater for those who have no access to the other side of the language barrier themselves but require information from that source. The translator, as socially recognized expert, is acknowledged as possessing the special competence to convey information from one sign system to another. In conditions where individual translators cannot easily be dispensed with, because alternatives are unavailable or too expensive, for example, the translator's clients have no option but to trust not only the translator's technical expertise but also his or her personal and ideological loyalty. The translator's power is such cases is symbolic as well as material. Loyalty may have its price, and may depend on whose side the translator is ultimately on. No less importantly, unless the client can rely on an expert control mechanism, he or she is not in a position to challenge the image of the unknown as constructed by the translator. The history of the role of interpreters in early European encounters with the New World (Columbus in the Caribbean, Cortés in Mexico, Jacques Cartier in Canada) furnishes abundant illustrations of the interplay between power, loyalty and self-interest in the relations between translators and their clients.

7

One of the major tasks of the researcher wishing to account for translation as a social practice consists in identifying and interpreting the norms which governed the translator's choices and decisions. The task extends to accounting, in given communities, at certain times or over a period of time, for the system of norms governing particular domains of translation and the discursive models which inspired the norms. The adoption, in specific instances, of certain models in preference to others informs us about the motivation and strategy used by translators in negotiating existing norms, the kind of text they were aiming to produce, the goals they were trying to achieve, and the negative models they were presumably trying to avoid. The discourse about translation, whether by translators themselves or by others (clients, publishers, critics, readers), will also point up notions of correctness, operational aspects of norms and positive and negative models and prototypes. As was already pointed out by Toury,[26] establishing the nature of the relation of this meta-discourse, i.e. the historical metalanguage of translation, to the contemporary production of translations is a particularly delicate aspect the researcher's task. All this amounts to a comprehensive programme for historical research.

The task may still sound relatively simple. It is not, for obvious reasons. Norms are not directly observable, and there may be a gulf separating statements about norms from norm-governed behaviour. Tracing actual decisions and regularities does not tell us why the decisions were made and what induced the regularities. Moreover, cultural systems are extremely complex and perpetually changing entities, embedded in other social systems, each with a history of its own. Translation is necessarily anchored in several of these systems at once. We can therefore expect to find a variety of competing, conflicting and overlapping norms and models which pertain to a whole array of other social domains. Their directive force will in each case depend on their nature and scope, on their relative weight, their centrality or marginality, their relation to other canonical or non-canonical models and norms. This is what determines, for both collectives and individuals, the modalities of normative force: what *must* be said, what *must not* be said, what *may* be said, what *can* be said (see Figures 3.1 and 3.2 above). But these various obligations and prohibitions in turn correlate with modalities of normative control (Figure 3.3 above), which are based on relations of power. It is only within such complexes that we can begin to assess the role of norms and models as opportunities or constraints, and the translator's activity as being both pressure-driven and goal-seeking at the same time.

The fact, moreover, that in certain domains, at certain times, certain models, rules and norms are more in evidence than others, is a reminder of the hierarchies of power and of the (real or symbolic) power struggles that run through human societies. As social and cultural hierarchies change, new values, ideologies and structures prevail, and new forms of control, competition or patronage emerge, the models, norms and rules of translation change as well. As a social and cultural activity, translation is part of these structures and constitutes an operative force in them. It is precisely through the specific orchestration of translations, through the models which individual translators choose to adopt, through their assessment and interpretation of norms and rules, that they take part in that dynamic. In other words, the identification of the translator's models and norms and the appreciation of their relative strength provides access to, and insight into, strategies and motivations. It also makes of the translator an agent, an active participant in a complex exchange, a person with a particular expertise and hence a certain amount of power, and with all manner of private and public interests to look after.

8

The observation (above) that translation is necessarily anchored in several of these systems at once, reflects the fact that translations are not normally produced for their own sake, but for a purpose, and with reference to already extant texts and discourses. The normal mode of existence of a translation is not as 'a translation' or 'a translated text' *per se*, but as a translated legal document, a translated philosophical treatise, a translated work of literature. Rather than occurring in a self-contained universe, translations are inserted into – or sometimes between, or alongside – existing discursive forms and practices. In catering for the needs of the system recipient, translation cannot but defer to the prevailing discourses of that system. It is this aspect of translation which Tejaswini Niranjana calls the *overdetermination* of translation. As she puts it, 'translation comes into being overdetermined by religious, racial, sexual and economic discourses', and consequently she regards the deployment of translation in a colonial context as part of the 'technology of colonial domination'.[27]

Niranjana also takes the empirical study of translation to task for not thinking through the ideological and social force of translation, as in the case of its complicity in the European colonial project. This type of investigation, she charges, 'seems to ignore not just the power relations informing translation but also the historicity or effective history of translated texts'.[28] Criticizing in particular Gideon Toury's insistence on systematic, empirical description she observes that '[t]he 'empirical science' of translation comes into being through the repression of the asymmetrical relations of power that inform the relations between languages'.[29]

The criticism has some substance to it, if only because, coming as it does from a politically committed position, it draws out the political and ideological implications of the academic and scholarly discourse on translation, indeed of any discourse. But surely the main issue is different, and it is not so much that in the last ten years or so empirical translation studies have, by and large, and increasingly so, begun to pay attention to the fact that translation is bound up in relations of power – witness, for example, the work of André Lefevere, José Lambert, Susan Bassnett, Maria Tymoczko, Theresa Hyun and others working within the so-called target-oriented paradigm. The point is, rather, that empirical studies have yet to develop a comprehensive theoretical and methodological framework that can encompass the social and ideological embedding and impact of translation. André Lefevere's triad of ideology, poetics and patronage as determining factors in translation directly addresses the problem.[30] Niranjana's notion of the overdetermination of translation is a particularly useful concept in this respect, even though her book as a whole is too much focused on the colonial and postcolonial conditions and on poststructuralist critiques to provide a general framework.

As is being suggested here, an approach to translation via the issue of norms can furnish a key component of such a framework. It can cope with the overdetermination of translation precisely because the norm concept has its basis in social interaction, and therefore in questions of ideology, social complexity, shared values and the unequal distribution of power. Leaving aside the irony that it was, of all people, Gideon Toury who introduced the concept of norms into translation studies, it remains true that the broader theoretical and methodological implications of the norms approach need developing. One aspect of this concerns the very determination of what constitutes translation, and for whom. The following pages are a first, faltering step in that direction.

9

The complex of translational rules and norms operative in a particular community defines what *is* translation for that community, because it determines what is recognized as translation. The norms of translation broadly prescribe what can and should be selected, how the material is to be handled by individual translators, and how it is likely to be received. In this sense norms define the contours of translation as a recognized, social category.

It is useful to distinguish, as others have done,[31] between 'constitutive' and 'regulative' norms and rules of translation. The distinction is certainly not absolute, as constitutive norms cannot do without regulative norms and vice versa.[32] Nevertheless, we could say that, for a given community, the constitutive norms of translation mark the boundary between what is translation and what is not, i.e. between what a given community regards and accepts as translation and therefore agrees to call translation, and those modes of expression and of textual production or transformation which go by some other name (creative writing, imitation, adaptation, plagiarism, burlesque, etc.). Regulative norms of translation distinguish, within the domain called translation, between optional forms of behaviour. Particular options may be regarded as appropriate in certain types of cases, and the translator's perceived success or failure in adhering to this or that norm may be deemed to have resulted in 'good' or 'bad' translations. The regulative norms of translation are therefore subordinated to the constitutive norms. Regardless of whether a particular performance is judged good or bad, splendid or poor, it remains within the bounds of translation. Of course, serious or repeated breaches of strong regulative norms may still lead to the verdict that the product in question is 'not a proper translation', 'not acceptable as a translation', 'no longer translation', and so on, but this merely indicates that as regards translation the distinction between constitutive and regulative norms is not hard and fast, or uniformly used in different sections of a community. But if the outer edges of the domain of translation are often frayed, its centre is usually much more stable, and governed by institutionalized norms and rules. The canonical models of translation, moreover, are likely to serve both as archetypal instances of translation as such (hence satisfying the constitutive norms), and as examples of translation deemed excellent (hence satisfying the dominant regulative norms).

Nevertheless, the distinction is still useful in a number of ways. In fact we constantly appeal, however indirectly, to a constitutive norm to determine what our culture understands as translation.

In 1959, in his famous essay 'On Linguistic Aspects of Translation', Roman Jakobson presented a tripartite division of different kinds of translation into what he termed intralingual translation or rewording, interlingual translation or translation proper, and intersemiotic translation or transmutation. In Jakobson's own presentation of these different kinds, both intralingual and intersemiotic translation are 'translated' into other terms, 'rewording' and 'transmutation', respectively.[33] The very fact that the middle term is given as 'interlingual translation or translation *proper*', without a 'proper' intralingual equivalent (i.e. without rewording), serves as an indication that this form is the one which, in our contemporary usage, is commonly understood as being 'translation' *tout court*. In other words, Jakobson's extension of the term to intralingual and intersemiotic modes, accepted in academic circles as perfectly legitimate from a linguistic and semiotic point of view, acknowledges in its very designation of 'translation proper' for interlingual translation that as a social category this is what constitutes the entire concept of translation, to the exclusion of the other two forms. The formulation itself concedes that the extended meaning may claim validity in the academic community, but that it does not coincide with common usage. At the same time, in extending the 'commonsense' concept of translation to accommodate a number of related operations, the definition significantly *underdetermines* that concept. But it is equally obvious that the commonsense notion of translation as restricted to interlingual operations rests on the application of a constitutive norm.

The boundaries of what is recognized as translation can also be illustrated with reference to 'phonemic' translations (or transpositions, or whatever) such as the Englishings of Catullus by Louis and Celia Zukofsky, or Ernst Jandl's versions of Wordsworth.[34] A good many readers and critics have hesitated to call these texts 'translations', even though at least the Zukofsky versions were presented as such. However, the privileging of sound over sense in such 'phonemic' renderings is so strong that most critics[35] feel the result cannot be reconciled with our expectations of the kind of relation a translation should entertain with its original. The normative moment in this expectation is clear enough and appears in statements to the effect that translation *should* preserve such things as the 'sense', or the 'pragmatic meaning', or the 'communicative value' of the source text. At the same time, it is hardly a coincidence that renderings with an ambivalent status occur precisely in the literary field, with its relatively weak modalities of normative force and normative control.

10

Can we determine what constitutes 'translation' in, say, the Western world? In this crude form the question is obviously unanswerable. It needs to be broken down into genres, cultural circuits, geographical areas, and historical periods. In principle, and with luck, empirical investigation may then come up with at least partial answers in the form of shared assumptions and expectations, and hence shared norms and conventions. This is the type of empirical approach which was adopted, for example, by Siegfried Schmidt in his enquiry into the 'macro-conventions' governing the concept of literature as a social construct in West Germany in 1980.[36] As regards translation, certain intuitive formulations by seasoned observers may or may not come close to capturing a consensus in particular subdivisions, and could inform working hypotheses. With reference to modern professional interpreting, for instance, Brian Harris posits the existence of a 'fundamental and universal' norm, which is

> the 'true interpreter' norm, or . . . the norm of the 'honest spokesperson'. This norm requires that people who speak on behalf of others, interpreters among them, re-express the original speakers' ideas and manner of expressing them as accurately as possible and without significant omissions, and not mix them up with their own ideas and expressions. Occasionally this norm is made explicit, as in the oaths which court interpreters have to swear under some jurisdictions.[37]

Of course, just how 'fundamental and universal' a norm of interpreting is formulated here remains to be seen. But the formulation itself also reminds us that interpreting, as a mode of translation, is enmeshed in other spheres of human activity, and in legal and moral categories. They are part of the social construction of translation. At the same time, they mark the overdetermination of translation.

If this is true, it follows that decontextualized accounts of translation which describe the process without reference to its social environment, necessarily underdetermine translation. This was the case with Jakobson's description. It also applies, for example, to the semiotic definition which Gideon Toury offers as part of his broad 'cultural-semiotic perspective' on translation in Thomas Sebeok's *Encyclopedic Dictionary of Semiotics* (1986):

> Translating is an act (or a process) which is performed (or occurs) over and across systemic borders. In the widest of its possible senses it is a series of operations, or procedures, whereby one semiotic entity, which is a constituent (element) of a certain cultural (sub)system, is transformed into another semiotic entity, which forms at least a potential element of another cultural (sub)system, providing that some informa-

tional core is retained 'invariant under transformation', and on its basis a relationship known as 'equivalence' is established between the resultant and initial entities.[38]

Like Jakobson's, this definition presents a considerable extension of our 'normal', colloquial and/or intuitive use of the term 'translation' in much of the Western world today. In its attempt to extrapolate a minimal semiotic kernel from a large number of everyday, metaphoric and scholarly uses of the term 'translation', it clearly underdetermines the concept, at least in comparison with the 'commonsense' notion of 'translation proper'. Of course, it is the combination of modern academic discourses on languages and sign systems together with existing 'commonsense' concepts and practices of translation which create the conditions for the definition in the first place, and for its acceptance in an academic milieu.

Insofar as the definition isolates the minimal or core features of a particular kind of semiotic operation, it also intends to name a universal category, presumably 'translation' unbound by socio-cultural and other conditioning factors. This would be the common denominator abstracted from all those practices termed 'translation' in one language, *'traduction'* in another, *'Übersetzung'* in a third, *'vertaling'* in a fourth, etc. The definition is then the result of a progressive reduction to a minimal set of constitutive norms, i.e. the requirement concerning the retention 'invariant under transformation' of 'some informational core', and the consequent establishment of a relation of 'equivalence' (the terms are obviously problematical, as is the syntax of the definition as regards the 'equivalence' clause). Even if the 'providing' clause in the definition is read as a purely descriptive statement, the problem is only displaced, as in performing operations which might qualify as 'translation', cultures will still have to decide what they recognize as the *valid* retention 'invariant under transformation' of an informational core.

Just how broad or universal is the definition then? Clearly, the reduction of the translative operation to a semiotic core puts it at some remove from particular socio-culturally determined 'commonsense' concepts of translation as they occur in individual languages. Its claim to universality could then mean one of two things. *Either* all usages in all languages have a common core of meaning for their respective terms denoting 'translation', i.e. for whatever translates as 'translation' from and into the local idiom, although one must then wonder on the basis of what concept of translation the terminological and conceptual equivalence is to be established. *Or* the definition identifies a universal non-linguistic category, an operation denoted by means of different terms in different languages. This presents problems of a different kind, among them the question of knowing how terms in individual languages correspond to this entity.

Neither interpretation looks convincing or even tenable. However, even if we reject the definition's implicit – and never more than implicit – claim to universality, it will still be useful as a tool to explore other, and possibly very different concepts of translation in other cultures. Its virtue lies precisely in the fact that it clearly, and deliberately, underdetermines translation as it has been practised in much of the Western tradition. But it is worth remembering that in using the semiotic definition to approach concepts of translation in other cultures, the normative moment in the definition is retained. While this presents theoretical and philosophical problems, it is hard to envisage a practical alternative. When we attempt to grasp and circumscribe the concept of translation, and hence its constitutive norms, in other cultures, there is no safe, objective point from which to tackle the issue. In this respect the translation researcher's operations are similar to, and as problematical as, the type of 'cultural translation' performed by anthropologists.[39]

In looking at the field of translation in a distant culture – distant in time, place or ideology – researchers project the concept of translation prevalent in their own time, place and language onto the new domain, and start from there. This happens in other domains as well. Our present-day cultural categories have no exact counterpart in, say, tenth-century European societies, or among the Nambikwara of the Amazon region. If we nevertheless wish to study cultural products which function in those communities in a manner comparable in one way or another with what we here and now call, for example, 'literature', or 'art', we have no other option except to explore the possibility that something resembling our known categories, however minimally defined, exists in those communities, and subsequently to proceed from this assumption of commensurability to map and gloss the various practices in the other culture, together with their metalanguages, and together with related practices in the immediate vicinity. The exploration and delineation of the domain of translation in distant cultures is no different from this essentially ethnographic and heavily interpretive practice. The ethnocentric bias is undeniable.[40] Of course, similar procedures are applied in most historical investigations, and they, too, invariably bring into play the researcher's own preconceptions and historicity. The fact that, in the case of translation, the researcher's concept of translation cannot help being determined by the prevailing translational norms in his or her own culture and milieu, can serve as a reminder that the separation between object-level and meta-level is rather less clear-cut that we might like to believe. Moreover, when we translate into our own terms a concept of translation radically different from ours, we inevitably do so by making use of our own categories of translation.[41]

The exploration begins, then, by establishing a 'base of agreement' to make comparison and commensuration possible.[42] In the case of translation there may be something to be said for taking Toury's semiotic definition of translation as a starting point. Having grown out of the contemporary scholarly discourse of descriptive studies, it clearly underdetermines concepts of translation current in the Western tradition and may reasonably be expected also to underdetermine (many? most?) concepts of translation likely to be encountered in other cultures, communities and/or periods. Precisely because it underdetermines the social practice of translation, the semiotic definition serves to counterbalance to some extent the fact that the researcher's perspective is necessarily grounded in his or her own overdetermined 'commonsense' understanding of translation. This will facilitate the subsequent mapping and plotting of culturally different conceptions of translation as far as possible in their own terms and context.

What this amounts to, is an attempt to grasp and reconstruct the other community's culture-specific field of translation in its relation to its immediate environment, i.e. in its social conditioning and overdetermination. This is rather more than a simple matter of fleshing out a clinically decontextualized semiotic skeleton. As, for example, Clifford Geertz demonstrates in his essay 'Art as a Cultural System', the practices encountered in one domain of culture can only be understood in the light of the practices which make up culture as a whole. As he puts it:

> It is out of participation in the general system of symbolic forms we call culture that participation in the particular we call art, which is in fact but a sector of it, is possible. A theory of art is thus at the same time a theory of culture, not an autonomous enterprise. And if it is a semiotic theory of art it must trace the life of signs in society, not in an invented world of dualities, transformations, parallels, and equivalences.

The references in Geertz' article are to such art forms as Yoruba carvings, Abelam four-colour painting, European Renaissance painting, and Moroccan oral poetry. He might equally have been speaking of translation.[43]

Even so, the researcher's description of the assumptions, conventions, norms and rules of what another culture understands by 'translation' remains itself, necessarily, an interpretation, an attribution of meaning resulting in a textual construct, a cultural translation into the terms and terminology of one form or another of translation studies. As a scholarly text, and as a translation into scholarly discourse, the description, like other forms of cultural translation, is 'inevitably enmeshed in conditions of power – professional, national, international'.[44] Just as the terms of the process of transcription are neither neutral nor transparent but part of a broader conceptual and discursive web, so the product of that process is entangled in pre-existing structures and institutions with their own status, role and functioning. In other words, our own descriptions, being also transcriptions, are shot through with interferences stemming from the concept of translation inscribed in our own language and culture, and from our 'social persona', our position and position-takings (in Bourdieu's sense) in an institutional context. As a social practice, that is, the study of translation, like translation itself, is always overdetermined.

Notes

1. Jiři Levý, 'Translation as a Decision Process', in To Honor Roman Jakobson, vol. 2 (The Hague: Mouton, 1967), pp. 1171–82.
2. Gideon Toury, *In Search of a Theory of Translation* (Tel Aviv: Porter Institute, 1980).
3. *Ibid.*, p. 51.
4. See, for example, Armin Paul Frank and Brigitte Schultze, 'Normen in historisch-deskriptiven Übersetzungsstudien', in Harald Kittel (ed.), *Die literarische Übersetzung. Stand und Perspektiven ihrer Erforschung* (Berlin: Erich Schmidt, 1988), pp. 96–121; Mette Hjort, 'Translation and the Consequences of Scepticism', in Susan Bassnett and André Lefevere (eds.), *Translation, History and Culture* (London and New York: Pinter, 1990), pp. 38–45; Christiane Nord, 'Scopos, Loyalty and Translational Conventions', *Target*, iii, 1, 1991, pp. 91–110; Theo Hermans, 'Translational Norms and Correct Translations', in Kitty van Leuven-Zwart & Ton Naaijkens (eds.), *Translation Studies: The State of the Art* (Amsterdam: Rodopi, 1991), pp. 155–69; Theo Hermans, 'On Modelling Translation. Models, Norms and the Field of Translation', *Livius* 4, 1993, pp. 69–88; Andrew Chesterman, 'From 'Is' to 'Ought': Laws, Norms and Strategies in Translation Studies', *Target*, v, 1, 1993, pp. 1–20.
5. See, among others, Ladislav Holy & Milan Stuchlik, *Actions, Norms and Representations* (Cambridge: Cambridge University Press, 1983); Renate Bartsch, *Norms of Language. Theoretical and Practical Aspects* (London: Longman, 1987); Douwe Fokkema, 'The Concept of Convention in Literary Theory and Empirical Research', in Theo D'haen *et al.*, (eds.) *Convention and Innovation in Literature* (Amsterdam: John Benjamins, 1989), pp. 1–16; Friedrich Kratochwil, *Rules, Norms and Decisions. On the Conditions of Practical and Legal Reasoning in International Relations and Domestic Affairs* (Cambridge: Cambridge University Press, 1989); Hans Kelsen, *General Theory of Norms*, trans. Michael Hartney (Oxford: Clarendon Press, 1991); and Frederick Schauer, *Playing by the Rules. A Philosophical Examination of Rule-Based Decision-Making in Law and Life* (Oxford: Clarendon Press, 1991).
6. Mette Hjort (ed.), *Rules and Conventions. Literature, Philosophy, Social Theory* (Baltimore: Johns Hopkins University Press, 1992).
7. *Ibid.*, pp. ix–xi.

8. Friedrich Kratochwil, *op. cit.*, p. 70.
9. Anthony Pym, 'The Relations between Translation and Material Text Transfer', *Target*, iv, 1 (1992), pp. 171–90.
10. André Lefevere, *Translation, Rewriting and the Manipulation of Literary Fame* (London: Routledge, 1992).
11. See Hermans' 'Translational Norms and Correct Translations' and 'On Modelling Translation. Models, Norms and the Field of Translation' for further details and references to the theoretical works by David Lewis (*Convention. A Philosophical Study*, Cambridge, Mass.: Harvard University Press, 1969) and Renate Bartsch (*Norms of Language. Theoretical and Practical Aspects*) on which this view of the nature and role of norms is largely based. Hjort's *Rules and Conventions* contains critical discussions of the concept of convention as presented by philosophers like Lewis and Wittgenstein.
12. Edna Ullmann-Margalit, *The Emergence of Norms* (Oxford: Clarendon Press, 1977), p. 87.
13. Cf. Lewis, *op. cit.*, p. 97; and Hjort, *art. cit.*, p. 43.
14. Lewis, *op. cit.*, p. 78.
15. Bartsch, *op. cit.*, p. 126.
16. Schauer, *op. cit.*, p. 2.
17. *Ibid.*, p. 8.
18. Niklas Luhmann, *A Sociological Theory of Law*, trans. E. King and M. Albrow (London: Routledge, 1985 [1972]), p. 33.
19. The terminology is of little consequence here, and certainly does not imply rigid distinctions. As far as I can make out, writers on the theory of conventions, norms and rules do not use a uniform terminology. Individual terms derive their meaning from the other terms being deployed. In what follows I will often use 'norm' and 'rule' more or less interchangeably. On the issue of terminology, and its relative unimportance, see Schauer (*op. cit.*, pp. 14–5).
20. See Algirdas Greimas (*Du sens. Essais sémiotiques*, Paris: Seuil, 1970, 135ff.) and especially Dirk de Geest ('The Notion of 'System': Its Theoretical Importance and Its Methodological Implications for a Functionalist Translation Theory', in Harald Kittel, ed., *Geschichte, System, Literarische Übersetzung/Histories, Systems, Literary Translations*, Berlin: Erich Schmidt, 1992, pp. 32–45, and De Geest, *Literatuur als systeem. Bouwstenen voor een systemisch-functionalistische benadering van literaire verschijnselen*, Leuven: Katholieke Universiteit Leuven, 1993) for the use of semiotic squares of this kind in connection with norms; the terms 'modalities of normative force' and 'modalities of normative control' (below) are derived from Alf Ross (*Directives and Norms*, London: Routledge, 1968, pp. 177ff.), where they are discussed in a legal context, and in a different form. The horizontal axes in the semiotic square indicate relations of opposition; the diagonal lines, relations of contradiction; and the vertical lines, relations of implication.
21. Schauer, *op. cit.*, pp. 38ff., 165ff.
22. Charles Taylor, 'To Follow a Rule...', in C. Calhoun, E. Lipuma and M. Postone (eds.), *Bourdieu: Critical Perspectives* (Cambridge: Polity Press, 1993), pp. 45–60 (first published in Hjort (ed.), *Rules and Conventions*).
23. Ross, *op. cit.*, pp. 127ff.
24. For exemplary case studies cf. Richard Shweder, 'Ghost Busters in Anthropology', in Roy D'Andrade and Claudia Strauss (eds.), *Human Motives and Cultural*

Models (Cambridge: Cambridge University Press, 1992); and Dorothy Holland, 'How Cultural Systems Become Desire. A Case Study of American Romance', in Roy D'Andrade and Claudia Strauss (eds.), *Human Motives and Cultural Models*, pp. 61–89.

25. The parallel here is with Bourdieu's account of the acquisition of 'correct' linguistic usage in 'The Production and Reproduction of Legitimate Language': "'Correct usage' is the product of a competence which is an *incorporated grammar*, the word grammar being used explicitly (and not tacitly, as it is by the linguists) in its true sense of a system of scholarly rules, derived *ex post facto* from expressed discourse and set up as imperative norms for discourse yet to be expressed' (*Language and Symbolic Power*, trans. G. Raymond and M. Adamson, Cambridge: Polity Press, 1991, p. 61).

26. *In Search of a Theory of Translation*, p. 57ff.

27. *Siting Translation. History, Post-Structuralism and the Colonial Text* (Berkeley and Los Angeles: University of California Press, 1992), p. 21.

28. *Ibid.*, p. 59.

29. *Ibid.*, p. 60.

30. See e.g. Lefevere (*Translation, Rewriting and the Manipulation of Literary Fame*) for the theoretical exposition and case studies, and Hermans ('Translation between Poetics and Ideology', *Translation and Literature* 3, 1994, pp. 138–45) for criticism of both.

31. Nord, *art. cit.*; and Chesterman, *art. cit.*

32. Schauer, *op. cit.*, pp. 6–7; and Kratochwil, *op. cit.*, p. 26.

33. See also, of course, Jacques Derrida's shrewd and ironic comments on the terms and assumptions of Jakobson's division, in 'Des Tours de Babel', in Joseph Graham (ed.), *Difference in Translation* (Ithaca: Cornell University Press, 1985), pp. 165–248.

34. Lefevere, *Translating Poetry. Seven Strategies and a Blueprint* (Assen and Amsterdam: Van Gorcum, 1975), pp. 19–26; and Toury, *op. cit.*, pp. 43–5.

35. Including e.g. Lefevere, at least in *Translating Poetry*.

36. Siegfried Schmidt, 'Conventions and Literature', in Hjort, *op. cit.*, pp. 222–24.

37. Brian Harris, 'Norms in Interpretation', *Target* 2, 1 (1990), p. 118.

38. Gideon Toury, '[Translation]: A Cultural-Semiotic Perspective', in Thomas Sebeok (ed.), *Encyclopaedic Dictionary of Semiotics* (Berlin: De Gruyter, 1986), vol. 2.

39. Talal Asad, 'The Concept of Cultural Translation in British Social Anthropology', in James Clifford and George Marcus (eds.), *Writing Culture. The Poetics and the Politics of Ethnography* (Berkeley: University of California Press, 1986), pp. 141–64; and Stanley Jeyaraja Tambiah, *Magic, Science, Religion, and the Scope of Rationality* (Cambridge: Cambridge University Press, 1990).

40. The point is also made by Niranjana (*op. cit.*, p. 67), with reference to Derrida's critique of Claude Lévi-Strauss. In *Of Grammatology* (trans. G.C. Spivak, Baltimore/London: Johns Hopkins University Press, 1974 [1977], pp. 122ff.) Derrida discusses a passage from Lévi-Strauss' thesis, subsequently omitted from *Tristes Tropiques*, where the anthropologist remarks that the Nambikwara do not have a word for 'writing', although he quotes a Nambikwara word which he reports as meaning 'drawing lines'. The word was used by the Nambikwara when they were inscribing wavy lines using pencils and paper given to them by the anthropologists. Derrida's criticism focuses on Lévi-Strauss' translation

of the Nambikwara word as 'drawing lines' but emphatically not 'writing', the inference being that for Levi-Strauss it apparently cannot mean 'writing' because the Nambikwara do not have a tradition of writing in the Western sense.

41. Matthijs Bakker ('Metasprong en wetenschap: een kwestie van discipline', in Dirk Delabastita and Theo Hermans, eds., *Vertalen historisch bezien*, The Hague: Stichting Bibliographia Neerlandica, 1995) offers an ingenious and pertinent discussion (in Dutch) of the problematical nature of the transition from object-level to meta-level in descriptive translation studies (an approach, that is, which does not wish to define translation *a priori*, yet needs to translate that which it observes into its own terms), and of the resulting complicity between the researcher and the normative structures of his or her object of study.

42. Tambiah, *op. cit.*, p. 131ff.

43. Clifford Geertz, *Local Knowledge. Further Essays in Interpretive Anthropology* (London: Fontana, 1993 [1983]), p. 109.

44. Asad, *art. cit.*, p. 163

4 Culture-specific Items in Translation

JAVIER FRANCO AIXELÁ

On the Cultural Aspects of Translation

Translating is above all a complex rewriting process which has appeared in many conflicting theoretical and practical situations throughout history. If there is anything to be stated without any doubt about translation it is its historicity, which goes hand in hand with the notion of language and of the *other* each linguistic community has had throughout its existence. The fact that for any case and for any moment, translation mixes two or more cultures (we should not forget the phenomenon, which is far from unusual, of mediated or second-hand translations, i.e. translations of translations) implies an unstable balance of power, a balance which will depend to a great extent on the relative weight of the exporting culture as it is felt in the receiving culture, the one in whose language the target text is nearly always elaborated, and, therefore, the one that generally takes the decisions concerning the way a translation is done (beginning with the decision as to whether a text is translated at all).

In principle, a translation offered to the reader as such tries by definition to satisfy two basic prerequisites that Gideon Toury defines in the following way:

> Literary translation is a product of a complex procedure, inevitably involving two languages and two literary traditions, that is, two sets of norm-systems. Thus, the 'value' behind the norms of literary translation may be described as consisting of two major elements (which may easily be further subdivided):
> (1) being a worthwhile literary work (text) in TL [target language] (that is, occupying the appropriate position, or filling in the appropriate 'slot', in the target literary polysystem).

(2) being a translation (that is, constituting a representation in TL of another pre-existing text in some other language, SL [source language], belonging to another literary polysystem, that of the source, and occupying a certain position within it).

Thus, this 'value' contains requirements deriving from two essentially different sources often incompatible, if not diametrically opposed to one another. (In this connection, one might recall the semi-popular formulation of this opposition as being between 'reading as *an* original' and 'reading as *the* original').[1]

This demand of double 'loyalty' is expressed in four basic fields:

Linguistic diversity

Linguistic codes in themselves are arbitrary systems in which the function and meaning of each sign depend mainly on the sign's opposition to other signs, and not on a supposed objective relation of equivalence with the continuum we call reality. The notion of arbitrariness does not allow the possibility of two linguistic codes placing each and every sign on the same point of their respective scales. This type of anisomorphism has already been treated exhaustively by authors like Mounin.[2]

Interpretive diversity

Derived from the act of reading which any translation involves and which appears to be one of the most polemical factors in translation theory,[3] to the extent that in some cases, within the equation 'translation = art', it has solidified into a defensive position for those who question the possibility of a scientific approach to translation.

Pragmatic or intertextual diversity

Based on the expressive conventions for each type of speech, which differ in each society.[4]

Cultural diversity

Plus its variant, historical distance. I will focus on this type of anisomorphism in this essay.

Each linguistic or national-linguistic community has at its disposal a series of habits, value judgments, classification systems, etc. which sometimes are clearly different and sometimes overlap. This way, cultures create a variability factor the translator will have to take into account.

At present, there is a clear recognition of the fundamental role cultural transference plays in translation, a fact that becomes clear if we think of the presence of the term 'cultural' and its derivatives in a significant proportion of the modern literature on translation. Cultural asymmetry between two linguistic communities is necessarily reflected in the discourses of their members, with the potential opacity and unacceptability this may involve for the target cultural system. Thus, faced with the difference implied by the *other*, with a whole series of cultural signs capable of denying and/or questioning our own way of life, translation provides the receiving society with a wide range of strategies, ranging from conservation (acceptance of the difference by means of the reproduction of the cultural signs in the source text), to naturalization (transformation of the other into a cultural replica). The choice between these strategies will show, among other factors, the degree of tolerance of the receiving society and its own solidity.

Research in the field seems to indicate that in the Western World there is a clear trend, with the important exception of technical genres, towards maximum acceptability, i.e. towards what Toury above defines as 'reading as *an* original'. The choice is far from being innocent, even in the (frequent) case of translators who decide on what to do in an automatic way, i.e. adjust to the implicit or explicit norms of the 'good translator' that will guarantee the acceptance of their translation by, at least, the initiator and the powers that be (publishers, literary critics, etc.), who have the power to sanction whatever text type translators may be working on. A direct consequence of this strategy might be what Venuti terms: 'a labor of acculturation which domesticates the foreign text, making it intelligible and even familiar to the target-language reader, providing him or her with the narcissistic experience of recognizing his or her own cultural other'.[5]

However, at the same time we are immersed in an obvious process of cultural internationalisation focused on the Anglo-Saxon pole. The constant importation of consumer items (cultural and other) from English-speaking America does not just imply a growing familiarity of many societies with the Anglo-Saxon world view, but also a clear process of gradual acceptability of its values and specific cultural reality, apart from establishing a series of translation strategies which are later mimetically applied to texts from other cultural areas.

The first two 'laws of translatability' propounded by Itamar Even-Zohar[6] and later revised by Gideon Toury[7] state that 'Translatability is high when the textual traditions involved are parallel' and when 'there has been contact between the two traditions', understanding the term 'high' as the existence in the receiving pole of a repertoire of solutions previously accepted and expected by the target text readers.

It seems clear that these conditions have been complied with in the relation established between the United States and Western Europe over the last decades. In this connection it should be enough to refer to translation data for some countries. Thus, García Yebra[8] states that in 1979 a quarter of all publications in Spain were translations, and half of these were from English source texts. Venuti[9] speaks of very similar current figures for Italy, with the interesting addition that, if we restrict ourselves to literary texts, translation accounts for between 50% and 90% of published books, depending on the publisher. Things are rather different in the opposite direction: Venuti again states that between 1984 and 1990, translations account for 3.5% of the sum of published works in the USA and 2.5% in the UK.

Such a one-way influence[10] and such a crushing supremacy in the most popular media channels (up to 80% of the Spanish cinema market according to newspaper data in April and May 1994, when the conflict concerning the share of North American films in the European Union was at its peak) necessarily imply that the receiving society is subject to a progressive familiarity with Anglo-Saxon culture. Translators are of course affected by this process, which among other things increases the number of socio-cultural realities whose transference requires less and less manipulation to make them acceptable in the target culture. In this regard, the comparison between translators' reactions to the same 'stimuli' over time becomes very revealing. Thus, B. Bödeker[11] comments on the shift that has taken place in the translation of the word 'saloon' in several versions of the same work. In the earlier ones it was replaced by functionally equatable terms which were nearer to the German receiving pole in a cultural sense, whereas in the last two translations it has been transferred by means of the strategy of repetition or non-translation, thus sanctioning its entrance in the receiving cultural universe. In the same way, among the translations of *The Maltese Falcon* I have examined, the 1933 version offers a sports term like 'golf' in italics, underlining its exotic nature and, therefore, its English cultural specificity; whereas the 1967 and 1992 versions repeat the term without any sort of typographical warning, signalling doubts about its English specificity.

It seems logical to think that the exporting system stands in a position of hegemony over the importing one, which entails the massive importing of cultural items in conditions very similar to those obtaining in the original setting, although with some exceptions I will comment on later and which are mainly related to the nature of the cultural item, the genre and the average reader the translation is addressed to.

What I have said so far brings us up against the paradox already depicted by James S. Holmes:

> Among contemporary translators, for instance, there would seem to be a marked tendency towards modernization and naturalization of the linguistic context, paired with a similar but less clear tendency in the same direction in regard to the literary intertext, but an opposing tendency towards exoticizing and historicizing in the socio-cultural situation.[12]

Holmes and other authors also state that the treatment of cultural items was almost the opposite in previous centuries. This change is usually explained as a development of the collective notion of language towards the idea of its essential non-universality.[13] Nevertheless, it must be acknowledged that this leaves us with no explanation for the apparent contradiction of such a difference of treatment between the linguistic and pragmatic planes on the one hand, and the cultural plane on the other, i.e. the contradiction by which current translations tend to be read like *an* original on the stylistic level and as *the* original on the socio-cultural one.

Culture-specific items are usually expressed in a text by means of objects and of systems of classification and measurement whose use is restricted to the source culture, or by means of the transcription of opinions and the description of habits equally alien to the receiving culture. In either of these cases, they are usually manifestations of a surface nature, outside the structure of the text. The linguistic and pragmatic levels, on the other hand, given that they are the materialization of the way of telling, seem to constitute one of the basic supports of the structure of the text, apart from presenting such a different codification that for those members of the target pole who are not bilingual (i.e. for the average reader of a translation in nontechnical text types) it would be almost impossible to perceive the aesthetic, informative, emotional or other aims most translations try to achieve, with the resulting financial loss for the initiators in a historical period characterized by a clear democratization of the commercial component of culture. Perhaps this is the field where we should look for at least part of the explanation of the disparity of criteria commonly observable in the way the three types of manifestations are translated.

Culture-specific Items

The first problem we face in the study of the cultural aspects of translation is how to devise a suitable tool for our analysis, a notion of 'culture-specific item' (CSI) that will enable us to define the strictly cultural component as opposed to, say, the linguistic or pragmatic ones. The main difficulty with the definition lies, of course, in the fact that in a language *everything* is culturally produced, beginning with language itself.

There is a common tendency to identify CSIs with those items especially linked to the most arbitrary area of each linguistic system – its local institutions, streets, historical figures, place names, personal names, periodicals, works of art, etc.— which will normally present a translation problem in other languages.[14] But the constant appearance of textual items which do not seem more arbitrary than the average, and whose nature as a translation problem can only be explained by appealing to an intercultural gap, forces the student of translation to widen his outlook.

In general, when speaking about 'cultural references', 'socio-cultural terms', and the like, authors avoid any definition, attributing the meaning of the notion to a sort of collective intuition. This option seems to have two main pitfalls: its excessive arbitrariness and, more importantly, its static character, parallel with the idea that there are permanent CSIs, no matter which pair of cultures is involved and no matter what the textual function (in one text or the other) of the item under study is.

If, in the present state of translation studies, we have learnt anything about translation and intercultural relationships, it is their dynamic nature. No two elements retain the same relationship over a sufficient period of time. Thus, if we seek a useful definition of a translation problem for translation studies and we maintain that only real translations can be studied, real translations will have to provide the criterion for the solution of the problem. As M. Snell-Hornby states:

> . . . the problems do not depend on the source text itself, but on the significance of the translated text for its readers as members of a certain culture, or of a sub-group within that culture, with the constellation of knowledge, judgment and perception they have developed from it.[15]

In other words, in translation a CSI does not exist of itself, but as the result of a conflict arising from any linguistically represented reference in a source text which, when transferred to a target language, poses a translation problem due to the nonexistence or to the different value (whether determined by ideology, usage, frequency, etc.) of the given item in the target language culture.

Let us give a few examples. In Bible translation, there is the now classic argument over how to translate the image of the 'lamb' into languages in whose cultures this animal is unknown or, if known, does not have connotations of innocence, helplessness, and so on. Thus, the translation of 'lamb' from Hebrew into the language of Eskimos will acquire, in principle, the status of a CSI and will become a translation problem. On the other hand, it will not constitute a culture-specific item, in its translation into Spanish or English, given its intertextually comparable load as a pure and sacrificial animal in the three languages.

Let us look at another example, provided by Frank & Bödeker[16]: the first line of *The Waste Land* ('April is the cruellest month [...]'). In the English tradition, we are told, April occupies the slot of lyrical month, and is associated with flowers and spring. In Germany (and in Spain) this place is occupied by May. The intercultural gap would be bigger (and have different implications) if the translation was made into a language whose intertextual tradition had April, for example, as the month of the most devastating hurricanes.

This is how a cultural problem in translation arises, linked to a pair of languages in use: a CSI to which translators will have to react somehow. They will act, consciously or unconsciously, taking as their starting point (to be upheld or transgressed[17]) the translation norms (genre conventions, intertextuality, credibility, interference, etc.) expected by their initiators, critics and/or readers.

In both examples there is another issue which must be discussed. Both CSIs are so in concrete textual situations. Coming back to April, a neutral reference to, for instance, the birthday of a character in this month would not, in principle, be a CSI as between English and Spanish (but it would be between English and a language which organized time in a different way).

We might try, therefore, to develop our attempt to define culture-specific items in terms of the above mentioned double tension any translation is subjected to: *Those textually actualized items whose function and connotations in a source text involve a translation problem in their transference to a target text, whenever this problem is a product of the nonexistence of the referred item or of its different intertextual status in the cultural system of the readers of the target text.*

This definition leaves the door open for any linguistic item to be a CSI depending not just on itself, but also on its function in the text, as it is perceived in the receiving culture, i.e. insofar as it poses a problem of ideological or cultural opacity, or acceptability, for the average reader or for any agent with power in the target culture. This fact certainly implies a flexibility which is not just unavoidable but desirable, if we wish to keep the notion of CSI open to intercultural evolution among linguistic communities. Thus, a third component in the nature of a CSI is the course of time and the obvious possibility that objects, habits or values once restricted to one community come to be shared by others.

On the other hand, if it is true that a CSI is only such in its textual materialization, and always from the point of view of the group that receives the message, it is also a fact that most linguistic items that appear to be CSIs in a concrete text are so nearly always, simply because their cultural differential tends to be synchronically stable between two given peoples, whatever their textual position. It is this regularity that has permitted students of translation to establish *a priori* categories of CSIs and make sense, and that will also allow us to establish and discuss the most archetypal situations in which these items appear.

Thus, we may distinguish two basic categories from the point of view of the translator: proper nouns and common expressions (for want of a better term to cover the world of objects, institutions, habits and opinions restricted to each culture and that cannot be included in the field of proper names.) From the point of view of current translating, most proper nouns seem to present the basic trait of adapting themselves in a very regular way to pre-established translation norms – which does not mean each one of them is always subjected to the same translation strategy, whatever the context and/or average reader. This is in no way an ahistorical fact, because at least in Spain in the beginning of this century there were heated arguments about, for instance, how English Christian names should be translated.[18] This type of proper name continued to be in a clear state of undefinedness until after the fifties, as becomes clear if we study the hesitations that still affect secondary genres like children's literature. We may find more proof of this development of translation strategies in, for instance, the established Spanish version of many of Shakespeare's first names, many of which are still real Spanish names due to their early entrance into our textual tradition (whereas, of course, current norms advise translators and interpreters to keep those same proper nouns in their English form when they come from a modern source unrelated to Shakespeare).

Following T. Hermans,[19] proper nouns can be divided in two categories: conventional and loaded. Conventional proper nouns are those 'seen as "unmotivated" and thus as having no meaning of themselves', i.e. those that fall under the collective perception we have of 'meaningless' proper nouns, apart from the possible textual or intertextual analogies authors – unfortunately for the translator – tend to activate. Loaded proper names are 'those literary names that are somehow seen as "motivated"; they range from faintly "suggestive" to overtly "expressive" names and nicknames, and include those fictional as well as non-fictional names around which certain historical or cultural associations have accrued in the context of a particular culture'. In the case of conventional names, there is nowadays a clear tendency to repeat, transcribe or transliterate them in primary genres, except when there is a pre-established translation based on tradition (important toponyms, historical fictional or non-fictional names like saints, kings, etc.). Loaded names have a much greater margin of indeterminacy, but they do seem to display a tendency toward the linguistic (denotative or non-cultural) translation of their components, a trend which increases with their expressivity.

CSIs which are not proper nouns make things much more complicated, and supratextual, textual or intratextual factors, as well as the nature of the CSI, acquire a much greater importance.

CSIs and Their Possible Manipulation

For reasons of methodological efficacy, I have thought it convenient to try to group all possible strategies applied to CSIs in translation. This classification is also ruled by an attempt to order them based on the degree of intercultural manipulation. Thus, we will obtain a frame which will allow us to discover quickly the general tendency of a translation as regards the double tension discussed at the beginning of this paper (being a representation of a source text and being a valid text in itself), which is perhaps the most important preliminary option when we want to discover the notion of translation applied in a text.

Like any conscious categorization of reality, mine is intended to have a methodological usefulness, and not to describe objectively any supposedly pre-existing classes. There will no doubt be border cases of a fuzzy or overlapping nature, which will have to be recorded as such. If there are too many, the validity of this scale of translation strategies would be falsified.

These translation procedures can be combined – and in fact are combined – and there is nothing odd in the same translator using different strategies to treat an identical potential CSI in the same target text.[20] But, on the one hand, there are many textual factors which have a decisive influence on the option taken in each case and, on the other, the relevant and representative element is the regularity of chosen options, whereas exceptions will act as modifying factors with an importance which will have to be judged from their textual relevance and recurrence in various target texts.[21]

I will try to explain the different categories and will add examples of English into Spanish translation from real texts, specifically from the three translations of D. Hammett's *The Maltese Falcon*. I will first give the English original, then a Spanish translation, and finally an English word-for-word retranslation, as long as this does not constitute a mere repetition or a slight variation.

The scale, from a lesser to a greater degree of intercultural manipulation, is divided in two major groups separated by their conservative or substitutive nature, i.e. by the conservation or substitution of the original reference(s) by other(s) closer to the receiving pole.

Conservation

Repetition

The translators keep as much as they can of the original reference. The obvious example here is the treatment of most toponyms [Seattle → Seattle]. Paradoxically, this 'respectful' strategy involves in many cases an increase in the exotic or archaic character of the CSI, which is felt to be more alien by the target language reader because of its linguistic form and cultural distance.[22] This reminds us of one of the paradoxes of translation and one of the great pitfalls of the traditional notion of equivalence: the fact that something absolutely identical, even in its graphic component, might be absolutely different in its collective reception.

Orthographic adaptation

This strategy includes procedures like transcription and transliteration, which are mainly used when the original reference is expressed in a different alphabet from the one target readers use. In the case of English into Spanish translation, it was a relatively frequent strategy until about the fifties, whereas at present there is a clear tendency toward maximum respect for English forms when there is no wish to translate them to pre-existing Spanish references. Nowadays, this procedure is reserved mainly for the integration of references from third cultures (Russian names in English works, etc.) and for the transference of Spanish words 'mis-spelt' in English texts.

Thus, in the translation of *The Maltese Falcon* by Casas Gancedo (1933), a Russian called in English Kemidov becomes Kenidof, whereas Calleja (1969) transcribes 'Jose', the name of the inscription (from 'Josephine', a friend of Hammett), as 'José', probably confusing it with this Spanish masculine name and, in any case, attempting correctness, one of the most pervading translation norms.[23]

Linguistic (non-cultural) translation

With the support of pre-established translations within the intertextual corpus of the target language, or making use of the linguistic transparency of the CSI,[24] the translator chooses in many cases a denotatively very close reference to the original, but increases its comprehensibility by offering a target language version which can still be recognized as belonging to the cultural system of the source text.

Units of measure and currencies are very frequent instances of this strategy [dollars → *dólares*; inch → *pulgada*, which is a unit not used in Spain]. In the same way, objects and institutions which are alien to the receiving culture but understandable because analogous and even homologous to the native ones, usually come into the same category [Grand Jury → *gran jurado* → big jury – a phrase which only makes sense in Spanish in connection with US culture, as there has practically never been any type of jury in Spain].

Extratextual gloss

The translator uses one of the above-mentioned procedures, but considers it necessary to offer some explanation of the meaning or implications of the CSI. At the same time, it does not seem legitimate or convenient to mix this explanation with the text. The decision, then, is to distinguish the gloss by marking it as such (footnote, endnote, glossary, commentary/translation in brackets, in italics, etc.)

This procedure is used all the time in the treatment of quotations in third languages and, traditionally in Spain, to offer data about famous people and to explain puns, which are usually termed 'untranslatable'. In the translations I have studied for this paper there is only one extratextual gloss linked with a CSI: [Arnold Rothstein* → * *Célebre gángster de los años 1920. (N. del T.)* → Famous gangster of the years 1920. (*Translator's Note*)].

Intratextual gloss

This is the same as the previous case, but the translators feel they can or should include their gloss as an indistinct part of the text, usually so as not to disturb the reader's attention. [five feet eight → *cinco pies con ocho pulgadas* → five feet with eight inches; St. Mark → Hotel St. Mark].

This procedure offers a variation usually due to the need for solving ambiguities, which is also one of the most universal traits of translation. I am speaking of what could be described as the strategy of explicitness, which consists of making explicit something that is only partly revealed in the original text (adding, for instance, the surname to characters only mentioned by their Christian names) or appears substituted by a pronoun.

Substitution

Synonymy

This strategy is usually based on the stylistic grounds linked with recurrence I discuss in the next section. The translator resorts to some kind of synonym or parallel reference to avoid repeating the CSI. Thus, in one of the translations of *The Maltese Falcon* we will study (Casas Gancedo, 1933), Spade appears in most cases repeated, in some omitted and in others by means of two main references: 'Samuel' (his Christian name instead of his surname) and *'El mefistofélico rubio'* → 'The mephistophelian blond'. In the same translation, we find that a repetition of 'Bacardi' leads the translator to replace the second reference ('He had drunk his third glass of Bacardi') *for 'Acababa de tomar su tercera libación del sabroso aguardiente de caña'* (He had just had his third libation of the delicious liquor of sugar cane), and the third, some distance away from the others, becomes a simple *'ron'* (rum).

Limited universalization

In principle, the translators feel that the CSI is too obscure for their readers or that there is another, more usual possibility and decide to replace it. Usually for the sake of credibility, they seek another reference, also belonging to the source language culture but closer to their readers another CSI, but less specific, so to speak. [five grand → *cinco mil dólares* → five thousand dollars; an American football → *un balón de rugby* → a ball of rugby].

Absolute universalization

The basic situation is identical to the previous one, but the translators do not find a better known CSI or prefer to delete any foreign connotations and choose a neutral reference for their readers. [corned beef → *lonchas de jamón* → slices of ham; a Chesterfield → *un sofá* → a sofa].

Naturalization

The translator decides to bring the CSI into the intertextual corpus felt as specific by the target language culture. Currently, this strategy is infrequently used in literature (with the clear exception of children's literature, where it also is beginning to decline.) [Dollar → *duro* (a currency denomination still in use in Spain); Brigid → *Brígida*].

It might be interesting to comment here that I will consider that historical persons with pre-established translations into Spanish (e.g. Queen Elizabeth → *la reina Isabel*) are not cases of naturalization but of linguistic (non-cultural) translation, as no Spanish reader would feel that these versions involve any sort of cultural substitution, because the name is still considered part of the source language culture (the person is still part of English culture, even if it is transcribed in Spanish terms to uphold tradition).

Deletion

The translators consider the CSI unacceptable on ideological or stylistic grounds, or they think that it is not relevant enough for the effort of comprehension required of their readers, or that it is too obscure and they are not allowed or do not want to use procedures such as the gloss, etc. They therefore decide to omit it in the target text. [dark Cadillac sedan → *Cadillac oscuro* → dark Cadillac; Casper Gutman, Esquire → *Casper Gutman*].

This procedure is used much more than many prescriptive translation scholars would like to acknowledge, as will be shown in the last section of this paper.

Autonomous creation

This is a very little-used strategy in which the translators (or usually their initiators) decide that it could be interesting for their readers to put in some nonexistent cultural reference in the source text. The translation of film titles in Spain seems to be one of the fields where most instances of this type of translation are to be found.

Among the texts studied for this paper, the best example – surprisingly a double example – we have is also the justification of the title of the book in Spanish (*El halcón del rey de España* → 'The Falcon of the King of Spain'): ['Shall we stand here and shed tears and call each other names? Or shall we' – he paused and his smile was a cherub's – 'go to Constantinople?' → *¿Que nos quedemos aquí derramando lágrimas como Magdalenas o que vayamos a Constantinopla en busca del verdadero halcón del rey de España* → Shall we stay here shedding tears like Magdalens or shall we go to Constantinople in search of the real falcon of the king of Spain?)

There are other potential strategies like compensation (deletion + autonomous creation at another point of the text with a similar effect), dislocation (displacement in the text of the same reference), or attenuation (replacement, on ideological grounds, of something 'too strong' or in any way unacceptable, by something 'softer', more adequate to target pole written tradition or to what could, in theory, be expected by readers). Attenuation seems to be the most promising strategy of those left out of my classification, and it is obviously used in the translation both of slang into Spanish and of secondary genres like children's literature in several countries.[25] In any case, the methodological usefulness of including these strategies in the scale will have to be determined by further study of real texts.

Explanatory Variables

The reasons that impel translators in particular cases to choose any of the above translation strategies can be very complex.[26] This section will try to establish a series of supratextual, textual, intratextual and 'inherent' variables the combination of which should help to explain the choice made by translators. The explanatory structure of the study will involve a series of steps which I will put forward in a logical order, from longer to shorter distance to each particular CSI. The various framing points are in fact interdependent and, thus, liable to modify each other in the up-and-down movement throughout the methodological scale which usually receives the name of 'pendulum approach'.

In the attempt to explain the possible reasons that lie behind the strategies, I usually speak of 'the translators' when giving potential motivations for the various strategies. It should be stated here that translators are usually the people who carry full responsibility for the product, but by no means the only ones who in fact control the results. There are people in authority like publishers, editors, proofreaders, directors, producers, other sorts of initiators, etc. who may change anything, usually to conform with what they feel to be social expectations. This, by the way, is a fact which gives even more support to the idea that the interpretive factor introduced by the translator is of a relatively secondary nature (at least in a statistical sense), because there are other agents who will bring into heavy discredit or who will not normally allow the publication of works which are too prone to break not only translation norms, but the linguistic and pragmatic conventions of the target language culture, especially in countries, like Spain or France, with a strong tradition of the notion of correctness in the written medium.

The following list is highly tentative. It includes what seem to be essential aspects for the understanding of any way of translating. Nevertheless, it is an open list in which the less important points may be dropped and where any important aspect can be added. The target texts will tell.

Supratextual parameter

Degree of linguistic prescriptivism

Is there any important group or institution devoted to the preservation of linguistic or stylistic conventions (e.g. Royal Academies of Language) in the target language? The answer to this question will give us new clues about the attitude towards interference or towards conventions like the naturalistic transcription of dialogues.

Spain is traditionally a very prescriptive country. This explains why until relatively recently there has been a clear tendency towards orthographic adaptation or linguistic translation of CSIs, conventional proper nouns included, for all genres whenever there were any kind of grounds, usually of an etymological nature, for their manipulation. This same control on the part of the Royal Academy of Language over the written medium helps to explain why translation for cinema, theatre and television tends to be much closer to real language than translation for written texts.

Nature and expectations of potential readers

Is it possible to define a group of addressees for the target text? Is the version planned for any special group? If it is (it need not be) we could understand the possible difference of treatment of one source text so as to meet the expectations, for example, of either teenagers or literature students. This same parameter, among others, could also help us to explain the reason for the special translation norms (very source-oriented) in English-Spanish of some technical text types, given the expectations and jargon of the specialists who are being addressed.

Nature and aims of the initiators

Are their aims in conflict with those of the translator or with those which are socially accepted? In shifting questions, such as the treatment of non-metric measure units, it is not unusual for a publisher to impose homogeneous translation norms[27] which transcend the idiosyncrasy of a translator, who will work in a different way when changing initiator.

And there is still another point linked to the demands of the initiator. Is there a publisher's policy that lays down special conditions for the genre or collection? For example, commenting on the translation of hard-boiled crime fiction or 'Série Noire' in France between 1955 and 1970, Clem Robyns[28] describes a collection with a pre-established length, which forced the translators to apply intense condensation or abridgment to the original texts, apart from the generalized deletion of opaque and ideologically loaded references. This is the same point that A. Kemppinen[29] makes when speaking about the translation of the romantic novel in Finland in the eighties.

Working conditions, training and social status of the translator

The more unfavourable they are, the more likely it is that we will have to consider the factor of unintentional behaviour or of bilingual and bicultural (in)competence. These are, besides, rather dangerous notions for the translation student, as they tend to come in a bit too handy when something is difficult to explain.

In many countries, literary translators complain (we certainly do so a lot in Spain) about working conditions that force them to translate very fast and with nearly no time for revision. These conditions, together with the lack of specialized training in a country that, like Spain, has not had a university degree in translation until recently, explain a number of incongruities and obvious misunderstandings. For example, one that appears in a translation of Dashiell Hammett's *Red Harvest*, where 'a parson named Hill' becomes '*un tal Hill*' (someone named Hill), because of a probable confusion between 'parson' and 'person', and not as the result of any sort of conscious decision on the part of the translator.

Textual parameter

Material textual constraints

The existence of some sort of image accompanying a text can have a decisive influence on the leeway allowed to a translator, as becomes clear if one compares dubbing with theatre translation.[30] In the same way, the treatment of CSIs in photograph captions has different sorts of constraints.

Previous translations

Previous translations of the same genre, author, or source text place constraints on the target text insofar as they have become a recognized part of the target language culture. As I have already mentioned, the existence of previous translations of classical works like Shakespeare implies that any reference to his characters is usually subjected to a process of linguistic translation that the same conventional proper noun would not undergo in normal conditions.

Canonization

Complementing the previous point, to what extent does the consideration of a work as a classic or simply as good literature increase the constraints the translator is subject to?

The non-canonized status of a text may cause, especially in very popular literature, a tendency to condensation (deletion of large portions of the source text) due to constraints of the target language system, which also explains the publishers' restrictions commented on by Robyns and Kemppinen in their papers. On the contrary, the 'literary promotion' of the same text will automatically require a much more 'respectful' (source-oriented) retranslation,[31] as in the case of Dashiell Hammett's *The Maltese*

Falcon into Spanish, which underwent a limited condensation in its first Spanish version (Casas, 1933) and which now receives a very conservative treatment as evidenced in two other translations of the novel.

The nature of the CSI

I have chosen the term 'culture-specific item' to stress the fact that a potential translation problem always exists in a concrete situation between two languages and two texts. When I speak of the nature of the CSI, I mean the type and breadth of the intercultural gap, before the concrete contextualization of the CSI takes place, given both intertextual traditions and possible linguistic coincidences.

Pre-established translations

In the same way as there are names of fictional and non-fictional characters and persons that have come into the intertextual tradition of the target language culture and whose treatment in translation will usually break the norm applied to those which have appeared more recently, the previous existence of a socially accepted translation of any CSI (as often happens in the case of important institutions and toponyms in the target language culture) will usually force a concrete translation (e.g. UNO → *ONU,* but UNICEF → *UNICEF,* and NATO → *NATO* while Spain was not part of it, whereas now it has become *OTAN*).

In this connection, the pertinent phenomenon will in fact be the deviation from tradition for the sake of some new translation norm whose increasing strength forces the change of a collective habit. Thus, nowadays the nationalist criterion seems to favour attempts to return to the 'original' term for toponyms, mostly when they are not too strongly embedded in the intertextuality of the target language; and more currently, the return to local language denomination – as the only official one in the whole nation – of some toponyms in near-federated Spain). We can find more proof of this in the shift undergone by phrases like 'Castle of St. Angelo' in the translation we shall study, where it became *'castillo de San Angel'* (castle of Saint Angel) in the first two translations (1933 and 1969) but *'castillo de Sant'Angelo',* in an even more Italian version than the original one, in the last translation (1992).

Transparency of the CSI

This is a factor which can explain many supposedly incoherent instances of translation. Translators who have chosen greatly to modify the CSIs may change their mind when a linguistic translation will be stylistically acceptable and easily understandable for their readers in target language.[32]

Conversely, the extreme opacity of the CSI offers a range of possibilities that goes from deletion, due to lack of understanding by translators themselves, to repetition, with the subsequent 'exoticization'.

Ideological status

A CSI may be shared by both cultural systems as to its existence, but not as to its use or social value. This can be an important factor when trying to explain shifts and deletions in which the translators change their chosen strategies to avoid inconveniences or redundancies which they feel their readers will not easily accept.

References to third parties

The references to CSIs belonging to third cultures are a special case in themselves and should be treated as such. Transnational CSIs (like institutions shared by several countries) are particularly interesting and usually have very strongly pre-established translations, as in the case of some abbreviations we have already mentioned.

In this paragraph we can also include references in the source text to cultural and/or linguistic items belonging to the target language culture. In some cases there are source text explanations about them which are natural (and frequent) candidates for deletion in the target text where, for instance, explaining that Seville is in the south of Spain could be felt as insulting to the average Spanish reader.

Intratextual parameter

Within the text, the treatment of a CSI also depends on the textual function it plays in the source text, as well as of its situation within it. The function of the translated item in the target text need not, obviously, be the same as in the original (beginning with the possibility of deletion), but there is a tendency that way, and the margin of freedom enjoyed by the translator will no doubt be influenced by it, mostly due to reasons involving the credibility and internal coherence of the translation.

In this connection, A. Kemppinen states that even in the case of massive condensations like those required of translators of romantic novels into Finnish, it is also expected 'that no unclear or absurd passages are formed as a result of omissions, that all names, incidents and points of time tally'. It seems obvious that this implies a selection of what is deleted, taking as the main criterion its relevance and/or recurrence in the source text, if only to achieve the maximum effect for the minimum effort – always with the exception of unacceptable items in the receiving textual tradition, as is shown by the fact that items like the transcription of dialectal variations tend to disappear in Spanish translations, whatever their importance in the source text.

Cultural consideration within the source text

In some cases, CSIs are also specific in the source text, as happens with many technical, minority or transnational references. It is therefore not too unusual to find intratextual glosses in the source text. This circumstance usually implies an important difference in translation, and in fact a clear candidate for, say, deletion might be kept for this reason.

Relevance

A factor that tends to influence the treatment of a CSI is its importance for the understanding and credibility of the text or of one of its passages. The textual centrality of a CSI will usually be a force that pushes the translator to give it the biggest possible degree of conservation (there may be other factors against it, such as pre-established translations or ideological considerations).

Recurrence

This textual factor is linked with relevance. The more frequent a CSI, the greater its chances of appearing with the highest degree of conservation in the target text (with the same reservations as in the previous case, and, for that matter, as always when one speaks about translation).

In addition, the recurrence factor offers an interesting variant linked with the stylistic requirements of the receiving pole. Contrary to the English-speaking countries, whose grammar demands constant lexical repetitions, beginning with the need to make the subject explicit in all sentences, in Spain – and in other countries[33] – one of the traditional parameters of 'good style' and something that has been and still is part of what readers demand of a text to make it seem *'an* original' is to avoid repetitions of loaded or unnecessary items too close to each other. CSIs are not at all free from this stylistic norm, whose effects manifest themselves in two basic ways: deletion and synonymy.

Coherence of the target text

When the translator has decided to apply a particular strategy to a CSI, its next appearance will usually receive an analogous treatment. Thus, we will often have to seek our explanation not in the present case but in the previous one(s), and even when the strategy is different, the previous appearance might easily be an important part of the explanation, as in fact happens, for instance, in the case of extratextual glosses, to which translators usually only resort the first time the CSI appears in the text.

Analysis of Three Translations of *The Maltese Falcon*

In this section I will try to carry out a brief analysis of the cultural manipulation undergone by one novel in three translations separated by periods of about 30 years. The volume of data I have obtained is clearly too small to allow general conclusions on the historical and generic level. Therefore, the aim of this study is to show that cultural manipulation really takes place, that in principle it is more marked in the field of common expressions (as opposed to proper nouns) and that translators tend to act in a way we might describe as systematic rather than idiosyncratic.

The versions of *The Maltese Falcon* (1930) I have studied are those translated by F. de Casas Gancedo (1933) [*El halcón del rey de España* ('The falcon of the king of Spain') Madrid: Dédalo, 1933]; by Fernando Calleja (1969) [*El halcón maltés* ('The Maltese Falcon') Madrid: Alianza Editorial, 1969 and Barcelona: Mundo Actual de Ediciones, 1981]; and by Francisco Páez de la Cadena (1992) [*El halcón maltés*. Madrid: Debate, 1992]. Henceforward I shall refer to them as Casas 1933, Calleja 1969, and Páez 1992 respectively. As I have done with the range of translation strategies that could be applied to CSIs, I will offer a word-for-word retranslation into English whenever I quote examples where the translation is not a mere repetition.

From a supratextual point of view, there is a very clear difference between the translation by Casas 1933 and the other two. Casas 1933 was published in a cheap paperback edition (of the type that is typically sold in kiosks instead of in bookshops in Spain), as part of a collection entitled *'Selección policíaca'* (Detective selection). Apart from mentioning the name of the translator and the author, Casas 1933 provides only the body of the text, omitting the dedication and any comment on the author or his work. This brings the work into line with all other detective stories, which have traditionally had a very low literary status. This treatment of the work as an instance of popular literature is clearly shown in two features of the translation:

(a) the great number of deletions of generally short and descriptive extracts, especially those in dialogues and those related to the abundance of spatial details which are so characteristic in the type of detective fiction created by Hammett; and

(b) the very curious tendency to 'warm up' the scenes with some sort of sexual touch in them (here is a sample: the short sentence 'She thrust her face forward and stared deep into his eyes' becomes *'Avanzó hacia él, mirándole con ardimiento, pidiendo caricias y amor con todos los movimientos de su cuerpo; [. . .]'* (page 193) (She advanced towards him, looking with ardour, asking for caresses and love with all the movements of her body), a strategy which seems to seek to increase the book's appeal for the average reader of this work, who belongs to a popular audience that has no time for literary niceties, details or complex characters, and that prefers its reading experience to be intense.

The other two translations are included in prestigious literary collections in the company of other canonical authors from various countries, Spain included. In principle, this places their audience in the middle-to-high cultural range. Calleja 1969 also includes a laudatory preface by Luis Cernuda, one of the most important Spanish poets of the twentieth century, which adds to the text's canonical status. Páez 1992 is a hardback edition included in a collection simply called 'Literatura' (literature), which also imparts some scholarly information about the author on the bookcover. In both cases, deletions are kept to a minimum, both in quantity and in the size of deleted extracts, most of which seem to be a result of absentmindedness or of the translation norm (as defined by the target pole literary conventions) that advises against repetition – though this last criterion is scarcely used in either translation.

This difference in publishing approach seems to suggest that hardboiled crime fiction in Spain has experienced a development in its cultural status or literary centrality, a process of canonization that, as I have already mentioned, would imply a shift to more conservative translation strategies *vis-à-vis* the original cultural world, as in fact happens in the translations I have studied here. This idea is strengthened in the translation of the title itself, which in the later versions is not only a direct translation of the English, but totally ignores the translation proposed in the first edition. If Casas 1933 had entered solidly into the central Spanish literary corpus, it would have been quite difficult to ignore such a pre-established reference due to the presumed familiarity of the Spanish reader with the title.

To end this discussion of the canonization of hard-boiled crime fiction, it may also be helpful to mention the nonexistence of a comparable genre in Spain until the sixties and, with any strength, the eighties,[34] whereas at present there are annual congresses on this kind of novel writers and the cultural supplements of the most prestigious newspapers pay tributes of several pages to figures like Hammett (cf. for instance, 'Babelia', cultural supplement of the newspaper *El País*, May 21, 1994).

To the factor of (non) canonization that completely justifies the intensity of deletions in Casas 1933, similar to those recorded by Robyns for the translation of the '*Série Noire*' in France between 1955 and 1970, we must add the historical perspective. For many years now, Spain has been a country strongly characterized by a very defensive attitude towards its language, with the (until recently) powerful Royal Academy of Language leading the movement in a manner that recalls the similar attitude of the French *Académie*, focusing its efforts on naturalizing all foreign influences as much as possible. This attitude, even though it has been in clear decline over the last few years, encourages deletion in the process of cultural domestication.

Finally, it is necessary to say that the cultural hegemony of the USA was just beginning in the thirties, and that there was not a specially intense contact or parallel evolution between the two cultures. Therefore, there was an important factor of unacceptability or opacity – the two are nearly identical in the case of most non-canonical works – in a group of CSIs that were then much more exotic than now. This is clearly shown in Casas 1933 by the shift to italics in terms like *golf* or *whisky* ('whiskey' in the original, also transformed in the other two into the much more transparent and recognizable 'whisky', but in roman type).

The fact that this study restricts itself to several translations of a single source text entails the advantage that most factors related to the intratextual parameter, and, to a lesser degree, to the nature of the CSIs, are identical for the three versions. The consequence of this is that the different treatments are much more directly linked with the translation norms for each period and with the attitude towards the source text as a more or less canonical text.

To describe the treatment of the CSIs, I have considered each different item with a specific cultural potentiality in the source text and I have quantified each CSI with a different treatment in the target text, including those deleted and autonomously created by the translator. In the course of this 'pendulum' process between the source and target texts, I have discarded repetitions of the same treatment of CSIs in the target text, on the ground that these repetitions would only adulterate the final results, as the percentages would be strongly influenced by the number of times key items like the names of the main characters are repeated.

Furthermore, the sum of potential differentiated CSIs that appear in the source text (226 for proper nouns, and 57 for common expressions) offers a range of possibilities that gives representative coverage to all the diversity of translation strategies which in principle can be used to solve this translation problem.

This method offers an additional advantage in that it also allows us to establish clearly the variability factor in the treatment of CSIs, i.e. the percentage of times the translator has resorted to different strategies to translate what, out of context, is the same potential CSI in the source text. This percentage is coherent with the comments I have already made about the three versions; with regard to the proper names (226 in the source text) we have 11.4% (255 differentiated treatments) variability in Casas 1933, as opposed to 2.6% (232) and 1.3% (229) in Calleja 1969 and Páez 1992 respectively; while for common expressions (57 in the source text), we find 14.9% (67 differentiated treatments) in Casas 1933 and 3.4% (59 different CSIs) in the other two versions.

We may estimate percentages of each translation strategy compared with the total of differentiated CSIs in each target text, and as we have just seen, this total is very similar in the last two translations which contain a somewhat smaller sum of different CSIs than that found in Casas 1933, where the important difference between potential CSIs in the source text and treated CSIs in the target text confirms that in this translation, cultural hegemony is granted to the receiving pole, as opposed to the much more conservative versions of Calleja 1969 and Páez 1992.

The conclusion based on the conservation/substitution of proper names and their breakdown into the different translation strategies is the great similarity in the treatment of proper names in the two later translations. It seems that translation norms for adult literature are extremely strong and coherent in this field, with a shift towards radical conservation that is usually placed around the 1950s in Spain.

Casas 1933 is a totally different matter. His 18.8% deletions of proper names (mainly the most opaque ones or those in secondary textual situations, i.e. those with a secondary importance for the understanding of the text or the development of the plot) is of great importance for the balance of conservation/substitution. To this we must add the fact that proper names with a functional load that transcends mere individual designation tend to disappear when they are opaque, or to change into common expressions (in a process of absolute universalization) so that they come to denote their meaning instead of connoting it (e.g. 'he did a short hitch in Joliet' becomes *'salió otra vez de la cárcel'* [he came once more out of jail] Casas 1933:128.) This procedure is also used in the other two translation, especially in Calleja 1969, but to a much smaller degree.

Finally, the remaining disparities between this and the other two translations are explained in relation to three more factors:

(a) the translation of Christian names of fictional characters who have 'translatable' names, understanding this last notion from the point of view of tradition, i.e. when the English name shares the same root with a Spanish counterpart, a translation norm that virtually only survives in secondary genres like children's literature in Spain. In that literature the strategy of naturalization of proper names can cover all proper names, whether they have a common root or not, showing once again that it is the receiving pole that dictates the norms and restrictions it is prepared to accept from the source text;

(b) the synonymy, exclusive to this translation (the other two resort – and then only seldom – to deletion to avoid redundancy), which also confirms the hegemony of the stylistic values dominant at that point of history in the target pole as opposed to those which appear in the source text; and

(c) the strategy of autonomous creation (five instances found for proper names and two for common expressions), also exclusive to this version.

'Common expressions' (as opposed to proper nouns) are much more liable to substitution strategies, i.e. to cultural domestication. In this connection, it seems useful to pay attention to what could be described as a sliding of translation strategies towards the cultural manipulation pole, most particularly in the two later translations, where we can perceive a clear shift of the dominant strategy, which was repetition in the case of proper nouns, and turns into linguistic translation in common expressions.

Casas 1933 chooses domestication and constantly resorts to deletion and to absolute universalization (more than 60% between both strategies) to solve the problems of cultural asymmetry between the two types of average readers – and these problems of asymmetry, we should not forget, must have been much more acute in the 1930s than now, given the lack of intense contact between the two communities. The result is that he introduces characters who eat, drive and greet, or have a type of relationship with authorities perfectly assimilable by the readers of his time, who did not have to make very strenuous efforts to enjoy the text as if it was *an* original, and, for that matter, the sort of detective 'original' they were accustomed to consume. At the same time, the local colour and, with it, the necessary (because commercial) dose of exoticism is still maintained by means of a much more conservative global strategy in the case of proper names. In short, we have a novel in which the reader – who in principle has no access to the source text – perceives its foreignness through most names of places and people, whereas the main characters move through those English-named streets and talk with each other using surnames which at least tend to be English, showing a type of behaviour which paradoxically (for us) tends to neutrality from a socio-cultural point of view.

The two most recent translations exhibit a high degree of mutual coherence, since they keep their global results within a 5% margin of difference, which is very similar to the margin shown for proper names. This seems to support the idea that the translator's idiosyncrasy acts in the field of particular solutions, but tends to be cancelled out when we consider the work as a whole because the dominant impulse is taken over by the translation or acceptability norms dictated by the receiving pole.

The treatment of common expressions in Calleja 1969 and Páez 1992 offers a degree of conservation of around two thirds of the CSIs, which even if much smaller than the more than 90% of the proper nouns – which are subject to much stronger tradition and translation norms – confirms the idea that the source text has achieved canonical status between the first translation and the later ones. Canonization, then, implies an increase in the acceptability of the restrictions posed by the source text, which become much more important to keep in the resulting target text, as long as translators salvage a minimum degree of comprehensibility for the average reader of their text. That minimum degree will vary depending on the average reader the translation is addressed to.

Let us finally compare a couple of significant examples. The phrase 'ate pickled pigs' feet' is deleted in Casas 1933, who simply states they ate together, whereas it is linguistically translated in the other two as '*manos de cerdo en escabeche*' (hands of pig in pickle) in Calleja 1969 and '*manitas de cerdo escabechadas*' (little hands of pig pickled) in Páez 1992. Again, when describing the form of the package in which the Maltese falcon finally appears in the novel, Hammett says it was 'an ellipsoid somewhat larger than an American football'. Casas 1933 resorts again to deletion, stating that it was '*un paquete de forma ovalada*' (a package of oval form); it is linguistically translated in Calleja 1969 as '*una pelota de fútbol americano*' (a ball of American football) and is explained by means of another CSI, i.e. subjected to limited universalization, in Páez 1992 as '*un balón de rugby*' (a ball of rugby).

The volume of data studied here is certainly too small to allow global conclusions about translation norms in any period, even for this literary genre. Nevertheless, this analysis seems to agree with observations made by other translation scholars like Lefevere, Toury or Even-Zohar, who suggest that the central or peripheral position of a work in the receiving corpus is a crucial factor in translation. Furthermore, it also confirms intuitions of the type that translation norms are, at least in Spain and in a few other countries, currently very intense and conservative for canonical works, and that the field of common expressions is much more amenable to cultural domestication. In any case, it should be clear by now that it is the receiving pole that decides in each historical period whether, and to what extent, to accept the restrictions that in principle are contained in any source text.

Notes

1. Gideon Toury, 'The Nature and Role of Norms in Literary Translation', in *In Search of a Theory of Literary Translation* (Tel Aviv: Porter Institute for Poetics and Semiotics, 1980), pp. 51–62; and James S. Holmes, 'Rebuilding the Bridge at Bommel: Notes on the Limits of Translatability', in *Translated! Papers on Literary Translation & Translation Studies* (Amsterdam: Rodopi, 1988), pp. 47, 50.
2. Georges Mounin, *Les problémes theóriques de la traduction* (Paris: Gallimard, 1967 [1963]).
3. Holmes, *art. cit.*, p. 51; and Mary Snell-Hornby, *Translation Studies. An Integrated Approach* (Amsterdam: John Benjamins, 1988), pp. 1–2.
4. André Lefevere, 'Why Waste Our Time on Rewrites. The Trouble with Interpretation and the Role of Rewriting in an Alternative Paradigm', in Theo Hermans (ed.) *The Manipulation of Literature* (London: Croom Helm, 1985), p. 239; and Dirk Delabastita, 'There's a Double Tongue. An Investigation into the Translation of Shakespeare's Wordplay', unpublished PhD, 1990, pp. 33–4.
5. Lawrence Venuti, 'Introduction', in Lawrence Venuti (ed.), *Rethinking Translation: Discourse, Subjectivity, Ideology* (London: Routledge, 1992), p. 5.
6. Itamar Even-Zohar, 'Introduction to a Theory of Literary Translation', unpublished PhD. Quoted by Delabastita, 'There's a Double Tongue. An Investigation into the Translation of Shakespeare's Wordplay', unpublished PhD, 1990, pp. xviii.
7. Toury, 'Contrastive Linguistics and Translation Studies', in *In Search of a Theory of Literary Translation*, p. 25.
8. *En torno a la traducción* (Madrid: Gredos, 1988 [1983]), p. 319.
9. Venuti, *op. cit.*, p. 5.
10. Basil Hatim and Ian Mason, *Discourse and the Translator* (London: Longman, 1990), p. 191; Julio Llamazares, 'Modernos y elegantes', *El País*, 13 May 1993, p. 15.
11. Birgit Bödeker, 'Terms of Material Culture in Jack London's *The Call of the Wild* and Its German Translations', in Harald Kittle & Armin P. Frank (eds) *The Interculturality and the Historical Study of Literary Translations* (Berlin: Erich Schmidt Verlag, 1991), pp. 65–9.
12. Holmes, 'The State of Two Arts', in *Translated!*, pp. 48–9.
13. Octavio Paz, 'Traducción: literatura y literalidad', in *Traducción: literatura y literalidad* (Barcelona: Tusquets, 1990 [1970]), pp. 9–12.
14. Peter Newmark, *Approaches to Translation* (Oxford: Pergamon Press, 1984 [1981]), pp. 70–83.
15. Snell-Hornby, *op. cit.*, p. 42; cf. also Toury, 'A Rationale for Descriptive Translation Studies', in Theo Hermans (ed.), *The Manipulation of Literature* (London: Croom Helm, 1985), p. 28.
16. Armin P. Frank and Birgit Bödeker, 'Trans-culturality and Inter-culturality in French and German Translations of T.S. Eliot's *The Waste Land*', in Harald Kittle

and Armin P. Frank (eds), *The Interculturality and the Historical Study of Literary Translations* (Berlin: Erich Schmidt Verlag, 1991), pp. 50–1.

17. Cf. Even-Zohar, "Reality' and Realemes in Narrative', *Poetics Today* 11, 1 (1980, 1990), p. 209.

18. Ramón D. Peres, 'Prólogo del traductor para la primera edición', in Rudyard Kipling, *El libro de las tierras vírgenes* (Barcelona: Gustavo Gili, 1980 [1904]), pp. v–xiv.

19. Theo Hermans, 'On Translating Proper Names, with Reference to *De Witte* and *Max Havelaar*', in Michael Wintle (ed.), *Modern Dutch Studies* (London: Athlone, 1988), pp. 11–13.

20. Holmes, 'Rebulding the Bridge at Bommel', in *Translated!*, pp. 48–9.

21. Delabastita, 'Translation and Mass-Communication', p. 206.

22. Holmes, 'Rebuilding the Bridge at Bommel', in *Translated!*, pp. 47–8.

23. Theo Hermans, 'Translational Norms and Correct Translations', in K.M. Leuven-Zwart and T. Naaijkens (eds), *Translation Studies: The State of the Art* (Amsterdam: Rodopi, 1991), pp. 163–4.

24. On the notion of transparency, cf. Newmark, *Approaches to Translation*, p. 78.

25. Nitsa Ben-Ari, 'Didactic and Pedagogic Tendencies in the Norms Dictating the Translation of Children's Literature: The Case of Postwar German-Hebrew Translations', *Poetics Today* 13, 1 (1992), pp. 221–30.

26. André Lefevere, 'Holy Garbage, tho' by Homer cook't', *TTR* 1, 2 (1988), p. 19.

27. Gaviota, publisher, 'Normas generales a tener en cuenta por los traductores'. Unpublished circular.

28. 'The Normative Model of Twentieth Century Belles Infidèles. Detective Novels in French Translation', *Target* 2, 1 (1990), pp. 23–42.

29. Anne Kempinnen, 'Translating for Popular Literature with Special Reference to Harlequin Books and Their Finnish Translations', in S. Tirkkonen-Condit and S. Condit (eds), *Empirical Studies in Translation and Linguistics* (Joensuu: University of Joensuu, 1989), pp. 113–37.

30. Delabastita, 'Translation and Mass-Communication', pp. 197–8.

31. Lefevere, 'Why Waste Our Time on Rewrites', in Theo Hermans (ed.), *The Manipulation of Literature*, p. 236.

32. Maria Antonia Álvarez Calleja, *Estudios de traducción* (Madrid: UNED, 1991), p. 226.

33. Gideon Toury, 'What Are Descriptive Studies into Translation Likely to Yield apart from Isolated Descriptions?', in K.M. Leuven-Zwart and T. Naaijkens (eds) *Translation Studies: The State of the Art* (Amsterdam: Rodopi, 1991), pp. 188.

34. Salvador Vázquez de Parga, *Los mitos de la novela criminal* (Barcelona: Planeta, 1981), pp. 291–5.

5 The Exotic Space of Cultural Translation

OVIDIO CARBONELL

Despite its being so recurrent in contemporary cultural and theoretical thought, the issue of translation as a paradigm of culture contact is not such a clear arena as it might seem at a first glance. Any survey of recent writings on cultural criticism will show that whereas translation is a fundamental commonplace in fields so separate – and yet so related – as linguistic theories of equivalence, comparative literature, history of ideas and cultural anthropology, the scope and significance of such a notion may nevertheless appear somewhat blurred depending on the context in which it is applied. It may well be the case that we still need a systematized theory of cultural translation as it is implied in any instance of contact between cultures, because, although there are a good number of seminal studies dealing with the subject, yet it appears that some reassessment is required of what is understood by translation in the framework of culture contact or the interpretation of cultures, before we attempt to approach such a problematic issue.

In the last thirty years, the field covered by translation theory has expanded from normative to descriptive studies, from a linguistic perspective towards a macro-level of study that encompasses the cultural context as a whole. Since the eighties, furthermore, translation theory has diversified substantially according to its different approaches. There is a trend in translation studies that analyses translation as a product; another trend theorizes translation as a social function; yet another – translation didactics – stands as a necessary normative development in translation theory.[1] But sometimes we find that the term 'translation' is used in a much wider, philosophical sense. When the most recent theories on anthropology or cultural conflict raise the broad question of translation between cultures, they are referring to semiotic or, rather, hermeneutic issues rather than to the purely linguistic problems of fidelity to the source text.

Contemporary cultural theory, therefore, deals with the relationship between the conditions of knowledge production in one given culture, and the way knowledge from a different cultural setting is relocated and reinterpreted according to the conditions in which knowledge is produced. They are deeply inscribed within the politics, the strategies of power, and the mythology of stereotyping and representation of other cultures. A pioneering study of translation in such perspective is George Steiner's *After Babel* (Oxford, 1975) which, in mapping out its own field, left many questions unanswered as to the conflictive nature of translation's intermediacy between cultures, and the relationship of the signifying processes that take part in translation, with the ideological context of the culture in which the foreign text is inscribed. Eric Cheyfitz, André Lefevere, Lawrence Venuti, Susan Bassnett are some of the theoreticians whose recent work deals with these relevant issues.

Primitive, exotic or Oriental texts provide some of the most illustrative examples of this bias. Let us try to select a paradigmatic example. If we are asked to choose the best known translation into English of the best known Oriental literary work, chances are that our selection will also include the best known (some would say simply the best) translator into English of Oriental and exotic literature. Richard Francis Burton's annotated translation of *The Arabian Nights* (1885–8) stands as a masterpiece of Arabic literature in translation as well as a monument of encyclopaedic scholarship. Yet the original Arabic work, a collection of popular tales from various sources, is hardly recognised as a valuable literary achievement among Arab scholars. Furthermore, the Arabic classical *qasida* has scarcely found its way into Western translation.[2] It is surprising, therefore, to read the following lines, taken from Burton's standard biography, written by Byron Farwell:

> The great charm of Burton's translation, viewed as literature, lies in the veil of romance and exoticism he cast over the entire work. He tried hard to retain the flavour of oriental quaintness and naïveté of the medieval Arab by writing 'as the Arab would have written in English'. The result is a work containing thousands of words and phrases of great beauty, and, to the Western ear, originality. Arabic, if we can trust Burton, contains the most beautifully phrased clichés of any tongue in the world.[3]

Here the figure of the translator/scholar appears as authority and cicerone to the unknown. But, as Rana Kabbani shows in her study *Europe's Myths of Orient*, Burton furnishes the image of the Arabs, and of Arab culture, literature, and even language, he wished to render, consciously or not: the image that was expected of the Orient and, of course, of his work as a translator. That image had been established long before Burton even set foot in Alexandria, as Said's *Orientalism* or Redouane's *L'Orient Arabe vu par les voyageurs anglais* remind us.[4]

Representation, stereotyping, strategies of signification and power: the network in which a culture is fashioned does appear as a texture of signs linked by endless connotations and denotations, a meaning system of inextricable complexity that is reflected, developed and recorded in the multifarious act of writing. If culture is conceived of in linguistic terms, the context in which a text is produced is of the utmost importance to any theory of cultural criticism that seeks to clarify the movement of signification that takes place in the semiotics of exotic worlds and alien spaces, real or fantastic.[5]

I find it useful, therefore, to start from some basic assumptions. Any approach to a given culture always involves a process of translation. Translation is articulated at various levels, of which the linguistic level (of semantic equivalence) may be adduced to be the first, or fundamental, one. Any cultural discourse may be said to constitute a text. As a consequence, cultural translation as a superior level of interaction takes place whenever an alien experience is internalized and rewritten in the culture where that experience is received. The handiest examples may be found in the anthropological and ethnographic fields, but in fact this rewriting is imperative in any case of cultural contact. There exists a gap between the significative context of the cultural components involved, there is always an element of untranslatability that allows the modification of the originary meaning according to the structures of representation of the target language/culture. This accomodation *in the interstices* – as we shall later examine[6] – is in fact one of the most important aspects of cultural translation, as it may also clear the path for the modification or even subversion of the existing canon.[7]

Translation, therefore, raises a number of issues fundamental to present-day understanding of our own culture in relation with other cultures. As *cultural translation*, it also plays a significant role in the questioning of received knowledge that has taken place recently in Western thought, largely as a result of decolonization. How to interpret other cultures; how to comprehend in an objective way what appears to us as the exotic Other; how to work out one's own historical reality and the other's; how to construe one's own actual cultural frontier; all these are questions whose background incorporates the broader issue of a *translation* between cultures.[8]

In the last few years, contemporary theory has dealt with these and many other aspects of translation at the cultural level. The so-called 'Manipulation School' in translation studies has developed a framework for the study of a text's relationship with determinate aspects of its cultural milieu, as well as the process itself by which a text is chosen and relayed in a different context. According to Itamar Even-Zohar, this cultural context may be termed a *polysystem*. He has recently proposed a theory of *transference* between cultural systems, which of course includes translational procedures. In his kinetic view of literature, language, and culture, negotiations between centre and periphery ensure the mobility of the accepted canon.[9]

The context involves not only surface semantic relations between both linguistic systems, but also the ideological and economic forces in the society at large. Similarly, the influence of functionalism, first, and deconstructive theories of textuality, later, has generalized the concept of translation applied to ethnographic discourse. The common antecedent is, of course, Walter Benjamin's reflections on translation as 'a somewhat provisional way of coming to terms with the foreignness of languages.' Ethnography may thus be viewed as 'a provisional way of coming to terms with the foreigness of languages – of cultures and societies'.[10] The ethnographer, as an interpreter making sense of the foreign, performs the same role as the translator, rendering the foreign familiar, and striving to preserve its foreignness at the same time.[11]

What are the causes and the consequences of this interpretation, this rewriting of the original (cultural) text, the position of the translator as a privileged cultural outpost? There are two key aspects that should be taken into account in the light of the structures of representation inherent in the process of cultural translation:

(1) the description of the processes by which the original cultural text (any cultural element coming from the source culture) is reinterpreted, manipulated and even subverted when incorporated into the target culture

(2) the possibility of a methodology in which meaning could be conveyed without usurping its original signifying function.

In the present article, I propose to examine the first of these aspects, especially as regards texts translated from *exotic* cultures; those in which there exists a weighty component of representation in the target culture, or in which the objective knowledge of the source discourse is substantially altered by a dialectic of attraction and repulsion. An examination of the reception and reinterpretation of Oriental texts in the light of recent theories of translation and culture contact will constitute a useful introductory exercise to the question of exoticism and the broader problem of multiculturalism on the present world scene. Given the abundance of studies on the subject, I shall try to assess how the structures of Orientalist thought exemplify the difficulties of cultural translation. The implicit construction of alterity in any recontextualization of meaning may hinder the understanding of any alien cultural text. As a consequence, the relocation of displaced identities in a heterogeneous common space is jeopardized.

It is traditionally assumed that translation poses more problems, that it approximates a higher degree of unassailableness, the more divergent the languages and cultures involved. Therefore, translation will be more difficult when there exists a tradition in which the source culture is represented in the target culture. Translation as a bridge between cultures may also be a source of separation when it reaffirms received stereotypes.

Recent studies have questioned the assumption that the accumulation of knowledge by one people about another constitutes a process in which objective truth is revealed 'through the disinterested quest of learning for its own sake'. Rather, knowledge is to a great extent determined by its pursuer, and especially by the relations of power that link the knower as subject as regards his object of study.[12] The most penetrating analysis on the representation of the exotic in the West is Edward Said's seminal study on the Orientalist discourse, *Orientalism* (1978).[13] Said's main argument is that the Orient is an imaginary space construed by the ideology, the cultural set of values and norms of the West: an 'imaginary geography' where the Orient is 'orientalized,' pictured as it ought to be, rather as it actually is.[14] In 'orientalist' writing, both the familiar and the alien coexist. The Orient may appear as a familiar world with aspects '*like* some aspect of the West',[15] but the strange, the distant and exotic seem to prevail over the familiar, at least until late in the 19th century. Yet, as P.J. Marshall points out, this was not the case in the representation of British India. Here, the familiar aspect was emphasized:

> In the case of the depiction of British India, the familiar seems to have displaced the alien and the exotic very much earlier. During the seventeenth and eighteenth centuries Englishmen increasingly sought to explain India, not in 'orientalist' language of its own but in terms that related it to the experience of western man. Relatively little was left that remained inexplicable by these terms. The challenge of an Indian exotic would be kept within narrow limits. (p. 53)

So, we learn, not only strangeness, but also familiarization, are two key processes in the interpretation of texts provenient from the so-called Orient (Jacquemond speaks of 'exoticization' and 'naturalization').[16] Said provides us with several examples of such strangeness, and so do several authors in the wake of his celebrated but also denostated volume *Orientalism*.[17] If we move further from the field of 'orientalism' ('Western' scholarship of Eastern cultures) and into the broader territory of Western representations of the exotic and/or Oriental at large, we will inevitably find the perennial taste of both the European reader and writer for stereotyped fictions of the Levant, the South, Moorish Spain and the like, as a correlate to similar fantasies of the Far East, unknown Africa, or primitive Indians or aboriginals. As is well known, nineteenth-century narratives of the exotic followed two closely related, albeit opposed tendencies that continue up to now: the attraction and repulsion, noble and ignoble savages, Golden Age or decadence, *maurophilie* or crusade. I have mentioned the conjunction of both tendencies, which is a necessary one, since both movements of representation spring from the same source: a projection of the (idealized) self onto the Other. This is the key argument of Said's assessment (the Orient is created, or *Orientalized*, made to coincide with European ideas about the Orient),[18] and its implications are profound and far-reaching. The narrative of the exotic is by no means exclusive of literature; it also involves serious works of scholarship whose claims of objectivity are challenged as a consequence. As P.J. Marshall puts it, the conclusion much recent writing has arrived at entails that 'an account of the accumulation of knowledge by one people about another is most unlikely to be the record of a progressive revelation of objective truth, achieved through the disinterested quest of learning for its own sake'.[19]

The most serious implication of these reflections is the near impossibility of acquiring a non-dominative, non-coercive knowledge when such knowledge is produced in a setting 'deeply inscribed with the politics, the considerations, the positions and the strategies of power'.[20] Speaking of an understanding and apprehension of the Other, we are thus dealing with the possibility of a Foucaultian subject-position 'from the outside'; the acquisition of knowledge of an alien culture without a seemingly inescapable mirroring of the self (in fact, Foucault has been a major influence not only on Said, but also on much postcolonial writing). We might be writing about culture without value connotations, of either Good or Bad, writing in a 'third language' of objective signification[21] that constitutes the neutral subject-position envisaged by Humboldt as a 'third universe' midway between the phenomenal reality of the 'empirical world' and the internalized structures of consciousness'.[22]

On the other hand, the fundamental question arises as to what extent, since quite a lot of Western representations of exotic entities are merely fictions of the Western mind imposed on actual peoples, are these peoples allowed to construct a selfhood devoid of Western assumptions and mythologies? Two examples may suffice. Traditional (Western) scholarship on Arab civilization has made explicit that any objective knowledge of this culture and its varieties cannot be achieved if we eschew the achievements of Western scholars since the eighteenth century. Yet, as Said points out in his essay, more often than not Western scholars stand as 'central author[ities] *for* the Orient ... put[ting] into cultural circulation a form of discursive currency by whose presence the Orient henceforth would be *spoken for*'.[23] The proportion of books on Arab affairs and culture published in France as surveyed by Jacquemond shows the great disproportion between books written in French, and the small amount of books translated from the Arabic and other 'Oriental' languages.[24] Any glimpse of scholarship on Islamic Spain, also a favourite field of research in Arab universities, confirms a similar perspective: apart from originary Andalusian sources (whose publication has been increasing steadily only since the Spanish scholar Francisco Codera devoted superhuman efforts to making available the resources of the Escorial library in the late 19th century),[25] hardly any contemporary Arab scholarship on al-Andalus written originally in Arabic is available in Spanish, French, English or German.[26] Cultural hegemony is obviously also echoed in translation.[27]

The second example has to do with the rise of nationalisms and Western modes of government in the so-called Third World countries. To what extent are nationalist movements firmly built on a genuine Indian, Arab, or any non-Western ideological basis? How are these countries to re-write their own history without incorporating a Western discourse which is therefore subversive to their own objectives? These, and many other commonplace problems in present-day thought, have at their core a fundamental issue of the production and transmission of knowledge, of relocation and the unfolding of the borderlines of identity between selfhood and otherness. This fundamental issue has to do with translation at all levels.

When the actual procedure of cultural transmission takes place, the linguistic, as well as the overall semiotic structures of the source (object) culture, are made to cohere in the light of the structures of the target (subject) culture. Rather than textual translation, a contextual translation takes place. A context is sought to be reproduced by making the linguistic fragments of the alien culture make sense, that is, fit into the context of the target culture. We should recall Talal Asad's assertion that 'in any case, the opposition between "a contextual interpretation" and one that is not contextual is entirely spurious. Nothing has meaning "in isolation". The problem is always, what kind of context?"[28] Asad's statement has to do with translation from an ethnological perspective. However, as recent research has demonstrated, the text, the context and the culture themselves are useful in the translation of texts from other cultures. As we have already mentioned, the self-image of any culture is construed in opposition to the image (the representation) of the Other, in terms of an all-pervasive *difference*[29] which stands at the very core of the process of the production of meaning. If we are to be aware of our own representations, stereotypes and mythologies, in order to better understand the experience of the Other, the way another person, culture or text handles the world, it is first of all necessary to perform an analysis of the information to be translated or culturally interpreted *from above*, that is, top down. Such an analysis proceeds from the macrocontext to the microcontext, from the text to the sign, instead of the *bottom-to-top* method of analysis current in translation studies (with a correlate in anthropology, ethnography or historiography) up to the sixties.

The important question of *equivalence* acquires further relevance once the contextual function of the translated text is taken into account. Inevitably, the translation is already a kind of given which the translator encounters. According to Venuti's comment on Benjamin:

> A translation canonizes the foreign text, validating its fame by enabling its survival. Yet the afterlife made possible by translation simultaneously cancels the originality of the foreign text by revealing its dependence on a derivative form: translation does not so much validate literary fame as create it.[30]

A translation will be accepted in the culture of destination according to certain traits in the context or climate in which the translation is undertaken. The text is chosen in the first place because the translator has *discovered* it in some ways. The circumstances of this discovery will mediate in the final recontextualization of the text in the target language and culture: the final refurnishing of the text's meaning.

It is a fact that eighteenth-century men-of-letters searched for objects of vicarious emotional identification,[31] either to detach themselves from traditional ties of allegiance to the established socio-political order and values of their own society, or, on the contrary, as a source of self-congratulation,[32] so as to underline or reaffirm one's own society's values and learning. This was the case when late eighteenth-century Englishmen accumulated knowledge about 'the history, languages, customs and manners of the people of India' in order to dispel its strangeness.[33] There is a motivation as to why the original is approached in the first place, and this motivation stems from the context into which the original is going to be translated, interpreted, quoted, epitomized or anthologized.[34] From the point of view of the contemporary poststructuralist concept of textuality, the relocation of the foreign text in a different context compromises its originality.[35] The concept of a linguistic sign as dependent on *différance* and opposition, in Derridean terms, that is, in the significative constellation of opposed references which constitute a language as well as a whole culture, but whose frontiers are never clear-cut,[36] prompts us to distrust the notion of linguistic and cultural equivalence. We face a major epistemological problem: whether communication between or knowledge about distinct cultures is at all possible.

It is obvious that communication and translation between cultures does exist. Nevertheless, contemporary poststructuralist theory points out the heterogeneous nature of the context of signification in both cultures. Meaning changes inevitably from source to translation; the intentions of the author and the translator differ and are possibly in conflict. To begin with, the corpus of source texts available to the 'Western' scholar is fundamental, as the sum of information conveyed from Oriental texts into Western texts is going to make up the representation of such cultures. When dealing with a culture whose language is particularly difficult to master, a (potential) complete availability of sources is only accesible to those scholars who have devoted years of study to, say, ancient Chinese, Akkadian or Arabic, and this same problem arises for non-European scholars who have to deal with European languages. This common scholars' dream is hardly attained. It stands to reason that not every text from every culture, ancient or modern, is translated, or even likely to be. For example, if we are dealing with medieval Arabic texts, the chances of their being translated will depend on whether there is a tradition of scholarship in the field, whether the subject of the text is of interest to the progress of the studies in the field, and whether there will be a fair number of works sold to a number of potentially specialized readers. The question of 'interest' is often related to, for example, national links with that culture (as is the case with Spanish scholarship) or, as in Great Britain, an element of exotic attraction not very far from colonialist attitudes.[37] In the Middle Ages, the establishment of chairs of Arabic in Western universities such as Paris, Oxford, Bologna, Avignon and Salamanca served the purpose of an eventual evangelization of Islamic territories,[38] an ideal not far from that of political dominance. The evolution of Arabic studies in Spain offers many examples of literary and historical sources reinterpreted so as to fit into the political climate of the age in which these texts were made available, either in annotated editions or in translation. A few examples: the question of the Islamic legacy has been a subject of debate in university circles since the sixteenth century, and it is still a preferred area of study due mainly to its far-reaching implications as to the nature of key aspects of European culture.[39] In post-civil war Spain, the discovery and interpretation of the Romance *kharjas*, supposedly the earliest specimens of European Romance poetry, or else examples of highly romanized macaronic Arabic verse, served to stir national fervour among Hispanists, Arabists and Hebraists alike, and the controversy is far from being solved.[40]

One may wonder whether the broadening of the scope of study by way of a rigorous scholarly training, and the use of reliable sources (both Western and Eastern) is enough to dissolve biased perspectives on a particular exotic culture. In fact, the privileging of some texts over others seems to be inevitable, as an assessment of the history of scholarly disciplines that deal with distinct cultures amply demonstrates. There is a 'spirit of the age' that determines the choosing of texts, the techniques of translation, and the analysis of data. For example, it is fairly easy to attest the influence of the aesthetic theories of the sublime and the beautiful in the interpretation of Oriental texts throughout the nineteenth century. The Romantic mood prevalent in the age also permits a classification of the Orientalist scholarship of Muslim Spain. There are 'maurophile' works which involve the representation of other worlds as models for totality – *looking at the past* (Golden Age myths, etc)[41], such as Thomas Rodd's translation of Ginés Perez de Hita's *Las Guerras Civiles de Granada* (1801),[42] Pascual de Gayangos's translation of al-Maqqarī, or the vast amount of English translations of Moorish romances (the Spanish Ballads) that were carried out from the turn of the eighteenth century. There are also scholarly works classifiable as 'Gothicist', the form of the Orient constructed (not only reinterpreted) as an oppositional image. These seemingly contradictory representations are, in fact, complementary. Both conform to dominant Western modes of thought: the idealistic and escapist representation of utopian space of moral consent and easy life, and the hypostasis of orthodox ideological, moral and aesthetic values. Despite their resemblance to the Oriental space that *is expected* to be found in them, the works chosen for translation do not convey radically disparate worlds. Rather than to *'lejanas y ajenas visiones'*[43] these works bear witness to our own close expectations of self-affirmation and/or change *within* the textual net in which we are entrapped.

In the last few years, there has been a beneficial increase in the number of contemporary Arabic works translated into European languages, largely as a result of university editorial efforts (P. Martínez Montávez, F. Arbós, M. Villegas, M.J. Viguera in Spain, among many others). However, we must be aware that despite the overall balanced approach that prevails among present-day trained translators from Arabic, there is an inescapable underlying tendency to select a particular work for translation according to its outlandish character or appealing subject-matter. Although we should praise the attempts at objectivity and fidelity of translators such as the late Marcelino Villegas, or Pedro Martínez Montávez, we should not forget what Richard Jacquemond has to say about the first translations of contemporary Arabic literature into French. His statement that 'the works chosen for translation were those that stressed the gap between the authors' modernist ideals and the 'backwardness' of traditional society (according to their descriptions)'[44] has a striking parallel in the translating activity of the leading Spanish arabist in the present century. Emilio García Gómez, who inaugurated the translation of contemporary Arabic literature in Spain, had specialised in Andalusian history and literature; his preference for medieval Spanish Arabs to the detriment of contemporary (obviously non-Spanish) Arabs is not unknown and, significantly, his only transla-tional incursions into modern Arabic literature are, as far as I am aware of, a translation into Spanish of Ṭāhā Ḥusayn's work *Al-Ayyām*,[45] and of Tawfiq al-Hakīm's *Yawmiyyāt nā'ib fi-l-aryāf*,[46] precisely the two 'modernist' works mentioned by Jacquemond as being the first Egyptian works that found their way into translation in France, and, therefore, also into Spanish.[47]

Samia Mehrez aptly objects to Steiner's exclusion of questions of colonialism and cultural hegemony 'in his otherwise classic work on translation theory'. In fact, when one comes to reflect on the implications of the imposition of the exotic model on foreign works made available through translation, one has to turn inevitably to the recent questioning of Western classic doctrines of cultural identity, 'humanism', 'universalism', and the so-called 'Grand Narratives' of the Western cultural tradition. The emergence, in a plurilingual and multicultural ambience, of postcolonial voices that are striving to rewrite their history as well as their position in the context of the Western canon, also confronts the issue of cultural translation. For their image is often conditioned by the reductive tradition of exotic representation dominant in the culture where they are now living, and which they contribute to change.

As we have already stated, exoticism constitutes a semiotic model imposed from *within* a culture from a one-sided, biased perspective. Any text imported into such a culture, or arising from within, is therefore handicapped: its significative network forced into an alienating fabric of dominant/dominated relationships. Such has been the case with translations of classical Arabic poetry as shown by Lefevere, or specimens from any 'exotic' culture, but it is also the case with ex-colonial literary or cultural productions at large. More often than not, the text is then submerged in the complexities of a many-layered cultural and linguistic context. Even if written in the language of the old metropolises, these texts reveal subtleties that belong in fact to another world: new meanings and new connotations that make up a different, 'hybrid' system of signification. Here translation takes place at a different level from that of linguistic equivalence. Meaning is not located in a source culture or a target culture in a univocal signifying movement; rather, it is being created endlessly in a third cultural space of growing conflict and complexity. Translating amounts to a difficult task: grasping these complexities, being aware of the differences with the models and standards of the original canon, issuing an affirmative movement that accepts the 'beyond' while being able to look at it from the outside. In other words: to be able to speak the language of the Other.[48] According to Khatibi, as quoted in Mehrez, this plurilingual reading experience often places us on the 'threshold of the untranslatable'.[49]

Samia Mehrez states that the very act of reading such *métissés* texts entails a decoding of a referential world in which more than one language is involved. If the postcolonial milieu requires such a translatory activity on the part of the reader *even when dealing with monolingual works*, whose context, nevertheless, is plurilingual, the traditional mimetic role of the translator is called into question. The translator's traditional *mimesis*, the usual considerations of fidelity or equivalence give way to a redefinition of meaning in which new relationships, new differences are fashioned. The reader as translator opens the field to new (different) representations.

Homi Bhabha's fundamental essay 'How newness enters the world'[50] explores this field of intertwining representations in the context of the emergence of postcolonial identities. The conflictual relationship between the colonializing and the (ex-)colonized object of knowledge is analized as each cultural subject organises the world and rearranges (translates) new cultural contents. Translation is defined by starting from Walter Benjamin's conception of the translation of meaning in the mobility between cultures[51]: as an internalization of knowledge, an understanding as well as an incorporation of knowledge, a far-reaching epistemological process that excludes the possibility of simple imitation.

Parallel to Mehrez's quotation of Khatibi above, there is one aspect in the process of translation that suits Bhabha's view of the conflictual representative world of the exiled, migrant or *métissé* subject. There is always a space of untranslatability, an element of *resistance* in Benjamin's words, where the cultural frontier is expanded, where the superposition of cultural layers negotiates the appearance of a new hybrid subject. This untranslatability sometimes results in the 'new' appearing as blasphemous (as in the Rushdie affair), and in the temporal displacement of the subject thus negotiated. However, it is in this intersticial passage where all processes of cultural difference come into conflict, and therefore become visible, that the 'migrant' historical experience (temporal and spatial) relocates its own self, creates a new fabric of cultural difference. The 'foreign element', cultural and therefore but not exclusively so, linguistic, becomes the element of change in any culture. Communication between cultures involves, by a translational process, not only a redefinition of the Other's meaning according to one's own representational context, but also a transformation of one's own articulation of representation, the construc-tion of a 'third space' of meaning that allows, for example, Salman Rushdie's personal redefinition of Indian history in *Midnight's Children*, or Derek Walcott's linguistic reinterpretation of the name *Omeros*, the inception of a poetic private language that echoes the idiosyncratic, hybrid world of Creole Antillean culture:

> I felt the foam head watching as I stroked an arm, as
> cold as its marble, then the shoulders in winter light
> in the studio attic. I said, 'Omeros',
>
> and *O* was the conch-shell's invocation, *mer* was
> both mother and sea in our Antillean patois,
> *os*, a grey bone, and the white surf as it crashes
>
> and spreads its sibilant collar on a lace shore.
> Omeros was the crunch of dry leaves, and the washes
> that echoed from a cave-mouth when the tide has ebbed.[52]

I changed Bhabha's expository order, and introduced a synopsis of his view of the translational activity in the migrant experience *before* returning to 'how newness enters' the world of the Self as the privileged subject of colonial enterprise, or of exotic yen and Oriental mystification.

Bhabha's central issue is an assessment of Jameson's rendition of the postmodern space of 'new world (b)orders'.[53] The famous Marxist theorist of postmodernity envisages a global, intercultural space where individual subjects are inserted 'into a multidimensional set of radical discontinuous realities'. In this fragmentation, cultural globality is to be found 'in the *in-between* spaces' (of spatial and temporal break-up), and thence 'the new historical subject' is to emerge from a 'third space' where new cultural practices and historical narratives are juxtaposed and originate at the same time. Bhabha criticises Jasmeson's description of a significative structure that, for all its suggestive description of interstitial cultural processes of signification, does not take into account the importance of historical displacement.[54] That 'third space' is the site of temporal/historical difference, the place 'where the negotiation of incommensurable differences creates a tension peculiar to borderline existences'[55]; the space of unstability where cultural translation takes place and becomes the medium of communication between different cultural realities. Jameson's momentous description of the cultural interstices in what he calls the new postmodern international culture lacks an appropriate assessment of the translatory movements of cultural representation. He dauntlessly directs his critical theory towards the emergence of a globality, towards the possibility of a historical narrative out of the fragmentation and discontinuity of individual subjects; but his efforts inevitably force his own representation upon other cultural experiences. Inexorably, these other 'migrant' experiences are denied their own constitution as legitimate subjects, the re-writing of their own history, the representation of their own experience, the construction of their own space out of cultural translation *at the interstices*.[56] Isn't Jameson here *familiarizing the exotic* as well?

As Jameson's 'thirdness' is developed according to the binary dialectics that result from his class analysis (that mark the distinction between inside and outside, base and superstructure), Bhabha reflects on the narcissism underlying the Marxist critic's scheme, which prevents the incorporation of communal identities dependent on other paradigms such as gender, race, or ethnic culture, unless these are subsumed in the totalizing, all-encompassing category of class differentiation:

> Such a narcissism can articulate 'other' subjects of difference and forms of cultural alterity as either mimetically secondary – a paler shade of the authenticity and originality of class relations, now somehow out of place – or temporally anterior and untimely – archaic, anthropomorphic, compensatory realities rather than contemporary social communities. (pp. 222–3)

So the 'third space' is inevitably defied and brought closer to the Self's 'first space' than to the Other's second one. Translation is thwarted by inescapable strategies of estranging (of the familiar) and familiarization (of the exotic). The processes of cultural difference allow desired knowledges that satisfies the narcissistic needs of the West, rather than the knowledge genuinely deployed by the Other (either the East, the Third World, the Primitive or even the Ancient).[57] What Jameson does not elaborate on is the subversive force that underlies the intersticial passage of cultural difference, the *analogon* where new identities, new texts and contexts come into being: the place where a constant and essential process of translation is relentlessly evolving.

Translation implies in the end the construction of a *sub-verted* text at all levels. My point here is that not only the source text, but also the target context experience the alteration infused by the translation process when their deeper implications are thus revealed.

Reading other cultures amounts to reading the *implicit* in alien cultures: 'If the anthropological translator, like the analyst, has final authority in determining the subject's meanings – it is then the former who becomes *the real author* of the latter. In this view, 'cultural translation' is a matter of determining implicit meanings'[58] ... 'This power to create meanings for a subject through the notion of the "implicit" or the "unconscious"' amounts to *authorize* them, the debate on ethnographic authority is formulated in these terms. But this also entails an *authorized* representation of the target culture itself: affirming, negating or destroying old or new stereotypes. The subversive force of translation lies in that the discovery of the implicit is carried out not only in the source text, but also in the target text. As Miller points out concerning exotic images,

> Given time, the image may often be assimilated and act as a powerful element in the self-conception of that same society, since the process is always a 'two-way' force.[59]

> *The negating activity is, indeed, the intervention of the 'beyond' that establishes a boundary: a bridge, where 'presencing' begins because it captures something of the stranging sense of the relocation of the home and the world – the unhomeliness – that is the condition of extra-territorial and cross-cultural initiations.*

> (H. Bhabha, *The Location of Culture*, p.9.)

Translation has been traditionally considered a mimetic activity. Although linguistic translation, linked to the hackneyed issue of equivalence, seems to aim at a redefinition of one text's meaning in another, at the reconstruction of an equivalent linguistic and semantic context, it in fact trascends the closed circularity of mere imitation towards the opening and expansion of the cultural field. Translation is a movement 'beyond', establishing a dialectics between here and there, now and then, us and them. And this expansive space where the processes of cultural difference take place, the interstitial 'space of newness' pointed out by Bhabha, is where the boundaries of culture are constantly being negotiated.

The bridge created from and with the materials of our own culture shares the same semiotic strategies of representation by which the 'other culture' is depicted. Yet, at the same time and by means of the strategies and the model so created, the other culture, the 'beyond', appears on *this side* of the bridge, albeit through the looking-glass of our representations, fashioned by dint of our translation tools.

Depending on the shape, colour and transparency this glass acquires, depending on the strategies that have been used in the process of translation from one text to another, the other culture will be more or less accessible, the shadow of its virtual boundary closer or further away, and more or less visible. As the quotation from Bhabha suggests, any creation of a boundary is a negating activity. Translation may make that virtual boundary real, or it may erase it almost completely, in which case there would not be any difference between the here and the beyond, us and them. A highly polished mirror may deceive our senses.

But translation may also operate from a space in-between, avoiding the negative activities of exclusion or homogenization. Writing in postcolonialism, an age of constant definition, contention and ambivalence, requires that the motives, the processes and the outcome of all translating activity be defined by translation theory, as one of the most relevant fields of any cultural project. Translation must be oriented towards affirmation, and that can only be achieved from that 'beyond' in the middle of the bridge between cultures. The uncompromising 'third space' of critical theory is the space of the only possible legitimate translation, as it is also the space where the cultural frontier is in constant movement, like the lace shore formed by the waves, hybrid of sand, foam and sea, in Derek Walcott's poems.

Notes

1. See James S. Holmes, 'The Name and the Nature of Translation Studies,' in *Translated! Papers on Literary Translation and Translation Studies* (Amsterdam: Rodopi, 1988), *apud* M. Carmen-África Vidal Claramonte, *Traducción, manipulación, deconstrucción*, (Salamanca: Ediciones Colegio de España, 1995), p.16.
2. See André Lefevere, 'The Case of the Missing Qasidah', *Translation, Rewriting, and the Manipulation of Literary Fame*, (London and New York: Routledge, 1992), pp. 73–86. The situation has slightly changed as regards contemporary Arabic fiction, partly as a consequence of Naguib Mahfuz's Nobel Prize award, but there are just a handful translations into English of the extremely rich Arabic poetry of the present century. See Richard Jacquemond 'Translation and Cultural Hegemony. The Case of French-Arabic Translation', in the same volume, for a prospect of the scene in France.

3. Byron Farwell, *Burton. A Biography of Sir Richard Francis Burton* (London: Longmans Green & Co, 1963) ed. Penguin Books, 1990, p. 366.

4. Edward W. Said, *Orientalism* (London and New York: Routledge and Kegan Paul, 1978); Joëlle Redouana, *L'Orient arabe vu par les voyageurs anglais* (Alger: Enterprise Nationale du Livre, 1988).

5. Classic studies on the subject of cultural representation from the perspective of difference are Tzvetan Todorov, *The Fantastic* (Cleveland and London, 1973) and *The Conquest of America: The Question of the Other* (a semiotic study, New York, 1976); Clifford Geertz, *The Interpretation of Cultures* (New York, 1976); Derek Attridge, *Peculiar Language: Literature and Difference from the Renaissance to James Joyce* (London, 1988). Due to the influence of poststructuralist thought, the number of works on the subject of difference has increased to the point that even an essential bibliography would cover several pages.

6. See Homi Bhabha, 'How Newness Enters the World. Postmodern space, postcolonial times and the trials of cultural translation', *The Location of Culture* (London and New York: Routledge, 1994), pp. 212–35.

7. The incorporation of foreign elements into the cultural discourse is of course a continual process; culture, as linguistic change, is often described as a constant flux. In a similar fashion, Lefevere thinks of literature as a 'stochastic' system of indeterminacies not necessarily adapted to a dominant ideology. Discourse opens the path for an opposed strategy, in foucaultian terms, and translation procedures *from within* the system may subvert and even transform the dominant ideology. See Lefevere, 'Why Waste Our Time in Rewrites? The Trouble with Interpretation and the Role of Rewriting in an Alternative Paradigm', in *The Manipulation of Literature: Studies in Literary Translation*, p. 225.

8. Translation has been recently related to the problematics of the cultural canon and its expansion. See George Steiner, *After Babel* (Oxford, 1975, 1992), pp. 486–95; Itamar Even-Zohar's various articles edited together in *Poetics Today*, vol. 11, no. 1, (Spring, 1990); André Lefevere, *Translation, Rewriting and the Manipulation of Literary Fame* (London and New York: Routledge, 1992); and the volume edited by Lawrence Venuti, *Rethinking Translation. Discourse, Subjectivity, Ideology* (London and New York: Routledge, 1992).

9. See his article 'Polysystem Theory', quoted above, and 'Translation and Transfer', in the same volume. I must acknowledge my indebtedness to África Vidal for making these texts available to me.

10. See Vincent Crapanzano, 'Hermes' Dilemma: The Masking of Subversion in Ethnographic Description', in James Clifford and George E. Marcus (eds), *Writing Culture* (Berkeley: University of California Press, 1986), p. 51. See also Stephen A. Tyler, 'Post-Modern Ethnography', and Talal Asad, 'The Concept of Cultural Translation', both articles included in the same volume.

11. *Ibid.*, p. 52.

12. P.J. Marshall, 'Taming the Exotic: the British and India in the Seventeenth and Eighteenth Centuries', in G.S. Rousseau and Roy Porter, (eds) *Exoticism in the Enlightenment* (Manchester: Manchester U.P., 1990), pp. 52–3.

13. Rousseau and Porter have pointed out that 'indeed a list of the controversies [that Said's book] has generated would in itself be a contribution to the 'history of exoticism'. Among the most significant of these, see C.A.O. van Nieuwenhu-jze, 'Palestinian Politician-Scholar Hits Back Hard,' *Bibliotheca Orientalis*, xxxvi, no. 1/2 (Januari-Maart 1979), pp. 10–26; Michael Beard, 'Between West and

World. Edward W. Said. *Orientalism,' Diacritics* (December 1979), pp. 2–12; Bernard Lewis, 'The Question of Orientalism,' *The New York Review of Books* (June, 24, 1982), pp. 49–56; Norman Daniel, 'Edward Said and the Orientalists,' *MIDEO* 15 (1982), pp. 211–22; Dennis Graffin, 'The Attack on Orientalism,' *Journal of Asian Studies* vol. XLII, no. 3, (May 1983), pp. 607–8; Edward W. Said, 'Orientalism Reconsidered', *Race & Class* 27, no.2, (Autumn 1985), pp. 1–15.

14. E.W. Said, *Orientalism*, p. 67.
15. *Ibid.* See also P.J. Marshall, 'Taming the Exotic', p.53.
16. Richard Jacquemond, 'Translation and Cultural Hegemony: The Case of French-Arabic Translation', in Lawrence Venuti (ed.), *Rethinking Translation: Discourse, Subjectivity, Ideology* (Routledge: London and New York, 1992), p.150.
17. Thus D. Sinor (ed.) *Orientalism and History* (Bloomington, 1970); Rana Kabbani, *Europe's Myths of Orient* (London: Macmillan, 1986); R. Schwab's *The Oriental Renaissance. Europe's Rediscovery of India and the East 1680–1880*, trans. by G. Patterson-Black and V. Reinking (New York, 1984); A. Hussain, R. Dison and J. Qureshi (eds), *Orientalism, Islam and Islamists* (Brateboro, 1984); Redouane, Joëlle, *L'Orient arabe vu par les voyageurs anglais* (Alger: L'Enterprise Nationale du Livre, 1988); the collection of articles edited by Rousseau and Porter *Exoticism in the Enlightenment*, quoted before, and many others.
18. See E.W. Said, *Orientalism* (1978), pp. 5–6: 'The Orient was Orientalized not only because it was discovered to be 'Oriental' in all those ways considered commonplace by an average nineteenth-century European, but also because it *could be* – that is, submitted to being – *made* Oriental.'
19. P.J. Marshall, 'Taming the Exotic', p.52.
20. Edward W. Said, 'Orientalism Reconsidered', *Race & Class* 27, no.2, (Autumn 1985), p.2.
21. Talal Asad, 'The Concept of Cultural Translation', p. 146; see also George Steiner's 'getting behind' of the translator, 'behind the language of the original with its local densities, idiomatic variables, and historical-stylistic accidence.' *After Babel*, p. 380.
22. *Ibid.*, p. 85.
23. *Orientalism*, p. 122.
24. Richard Jacquemond, 'Translation and Cultural Hegemony', p. 148.
25. Some relevant studies of the evolution of Spanish Arabism are James T. Monroe, *Islam and the Arabs in Spanish Scholarship* (Leiden: Brill, 1970), M. Manzanares de Cirre, *Arabistas españoles del siglo XIX* (Madrid, 1972). On the subject of Anglo-American scholarship on Muslim Spain, see A. Galán Sánchez, *Una visión de la 'decadencia española': la historiografía anglosajona sobre mudéjares y moriscos (siglos XVIII–XX)*, (Málaga: Diputación Provincial de Málaga, 1991), and my Oxford M.Litt thesis *Anglo-American Approaches to Muslim Spain: The Western Bridge* (unpublished, 1993).
26. See Richard Hitchcock, 'Hispano-Arabic Historiography: the Legacy of J.A. Conde', *Arabia and the Gulf: From Traditional Society to Modern States. Essays in Honour of M.A. Shaban's 60th Birthday (16th November 1986)*, ed. I.A. Netton, London: Croom Helm, 1986, pp. 57–71.
27. R. Jacquemond, 'Translation and Cultural Hegemony', p. 148.
28. Talal Asad, 'The Concept of Cultural Translation', p. 148.
29. Jacques Derrida, 'Des Tours de Babel,' in Joseph Graham (ed.) *Difference in Translation*, (Ithaca and London: Cornell U.P., 1985). Derrida goes as far as to

reject traditional translation theory, as the equilibrium between what is meant and what is said is irretrievably lost in translation; rather, a different significative structure, a new artistic work is created in the translation process.

30. Lawrence Venuti, 'Introduction', in *Rethinking Translation*, p. 7.
31. G.S. Rousseau and Roy Porter, *Exoticism in the Enlightenment*, p. 12.
32. Edward W. Said, *Orientalism*, p. 325.
33. P.J. Marshall, 'Taming the Exotic', p. 57; E.W. Said, *Orientalism, passim*; Rana Kabbani, *Europe's Myths of Orient, passim*.
34. See André Lefevere, *Translation, Rewriting and the Manipulation of Literary Fame*, London: Routledge, 1992.
35. Lawrence Venuti, *Rethinking Translation*, p. 7.
36. Jacques Derrida 'Round-table on Translation', *The Ear of the Other* (Lincoln and London: University of Nebraska Press, 1988, p. 100.
37. A study of the links between exotic attraction, translation and colonization regarding the image of the 'New World' is Eric Cheyfitz, *The Poetics of Imperialism. Translation and Colonization from The Tempest to Tarzan*, (Oxford and New York: Oxford University Press, 1991).
38. R.W. Southern, *Western Views of Islam in the Middle Ages* (Harvard, 1962), p. 72.
39. See O. Carbonell, 'Al-Andalus as a Cultural Bridge between East and West: The 'Arabic Thesis' Concerning Literary Transmissions in Western Scholarship (17th–20th Centuries)', *Al-Andalus: Centuries of Upheavals and Achievements*, (Riyadh, forthcoming).
40. See O. Carbonell, 'Hacia una gramática del caos. Reflexiones sobre la poesia estrófica hispanoárabe', *Foro Hispánico (Revista Hispánica de los Países Bajos)* 7 Amsterdam-Atlanta, 1994, pp. 39–59, for a survey of the main positions in the controversy, whose bibliography amounts to more than six hundred books and articles.
41. According to Daniel Miller, 'Primitivism, in its narrow sense, consists of the projection of social self-definition as a structure composed of being and otherness.' ('Primitive art and the necessity of primitivism to art', *The Myth of Primitivism: Perspectives on Art*, ed. Susan Hiller, Routledge, 1991, pp. 56–7).
42. Thomas Rodd, *Las Guerras Civiles, or The Civil Wars of Granada, and the History of the Factions of the Zegríes and the Abencerrajes, etc.* Translated from the Arabic of Abenhamin, a native of Granada, by Ginés Pérez de Hita, of Murcia; and from the Spanish by Thomas Rodd. London, J. Bonsor, 1801. See O. Carbonell, 'Ecos de historia romántica: la 'España mora' en Thomas Rodd y Washington Irving', *Sharq al-Andalus* 8 (1991), pp. 11–24.
43. M.J. Rubiera, *La arquitectura en la literatura hispanoárabe*, (Madrid: Hiperión, 1985).
44. Richard Jacquemond, 'Translation and Cultural Hegemony,' p. 151.
45. *Los días*, Valencia, 1954; first published in Arabic in 1929.
46. *Diario de un fiscal rural* (Madrid, 1955). Some of the translator's introductory comments are worth quoting *in extenso*. García Gómez tells us that the publishing organism (the Instituto Hispano-Árabe de Cultura, a branch of the Ministerio de Asuntos Exteriores) *'tiende a dar a conocer entre nosotros las obras que le parecen más bellas – y más 'comunicables'— dentro del campo de la literatura contemporánea del Oriente Medio. Es salvedad importante para todos. Los orientales no deberán extrañarse de nuestra elección, que puede ser errónea, pero que no es caprichosa, tiene sus leyes y no afecta en modo alguno a la categoria estética de algunas*

obras que de momento pueden quedar excluidas. Y el público de habla española debe asimismo pensar que lo que va a ofrecérsele viene pasado por muchas y diferentes cribas y que la calidad literaria, – que siempre se ha tenido, naturalmente, en cuenta – ha de ir hermanada, aparte otros factores, con el porcentaje de "comunicabilidad" de la obra que se traduzca.' (Ibid., p. vi).

47. See the comments on the French translation of these works, p. 151. According to Monroe, Garcia Gómez's role in these translations was important in that it inaugurates 'a new phase in Spanish Arabism,' carried out to a great extent by Garcia Gómez's disciple Pedro Martinez Montávez and his colleagues at Madrid's Universidad Autónoma.

48. Samia Mehrez, 'Translation and the Postcolonial Experience: The Francophone North African Text', in L. Venuti (ed.), *Rethinking Translation, Discourse, Subjectivity, Ideology*, London and New York: Routledge, 1992, pp. 121–2.

49. Abdelkebir Khatibi, *Amour bilingue* (Paris: Fata Morgana, 1983), Eng. trans. by Richard Howard, *Love in Two Languages* (Minneapolis: University of Minnesota Press, 1990), pp. 4–5, *apud* Mehrez, p. 122.

50. *The Location of Culture*, (London and New York: Routledge, 1994), pp. 212–35.

51. *Iluminaciones*, p. 69: '*la traducción entraña una continuidad transformativa y no la comparación de igualdades abstractas o ámbitos de semejanza*' apud *Africa Vidal, 'Los estudios de traducción'*, (forthcoming) p. 29.

52. Derek Walcott, *Omeros*, New York: Farrar Straus Giroux, 1990; bilingual ed. English-Spanish Barcelona: Anagrama, 1994 (Sp. trans. by J.L. Rivas), p. 24.

53. *Postmodernism or, The Cultural Logic of Late Capitalism*, 'Secondary Elaborations', pp. 297–418.

54. Homi Bhabha, 'How Newness Enters the World', p. 217.

55. *Ibid.*, p.218.

56. Several critics have pointed out that Jameson's tendency towards a global discourse of signification implies a political intention that reveals an implicit relationship between current (Western) structures of power. See Bennett for an appraisal of Jameson's 'aesthetic of cognitive mapping', and Robert Young, *White Mythologies: Writing, History and the West*, (London: Routledge, 1990), for Jameson's handling of historical discourse in the light of the representation of other cultures.

57. See Talal Asad, 'The Inequality of Languages', in 'The Concept of Cultural Translation', p. 158.

58. Talal Asad, 'The Meaning of Translation', p. 162

59. David Miller, 'Primitivism and the Necessity of Primitivism to Art', p. 60

6 Translation and Pragmatics

ENRIQUE ALCARAZ

1 Traductology and Translemics

'Traductology' and 'translemics' are currently two of the most widely accepted labels applied to the academic activity involving the deep examination of theoretical and applied issues of translation, although other names, like 'translatology', have also been proposed for this discipline. These two words, 'traductology' and 'translemics', to a large extent, cover the domain of a more traditional area of study known as 'translation theory and its applications', and of a more pretentious term like 'the science' of translation, though some people may feel that a term like *translemics* is more pretentious still.[1]

Some of the supporters of the latter term also suggest that translation is itself a science, although many more adherents to the concept of translation as an art could probably be found among the specialists in the field,[2] not to mention translators themselves, who seldom speak of the art of translation or the science of translation, but rather of the 'act of translation'. Whether translation is a science or an art seems to be a trivial discussion, since Ferdinand de Saussure taught us that *'le point de vue crée l'objet'* and, consequently, translation is fully entitled to be in the circle of scientific specialities if scientific procedures and parameters, such as observation, hypothesis-building, measurements of effects,[3] etc. are applied to its methodological inquiry. However, 'translation theory' as such is still a mere shadow in spite of the pressing concern of both linguists and philosophers in recent years.[4]

The investigation carried out by specialists in translemics and traductology has at least two main objectives:

(1) the persistent search for a solution to the problems of *equivalence* arising from the linguistic analysis of the relationships that exist between two

texts which, while conveying the same meaning, are written in different languages; and

(2) a better understanding of the *manipulations* brought about by translators in their earnest attempt to achieve this equivalence.

Two key words have been mentioned so far, *manipulation* and *equivalence*, 'manipulation' connoting 'linguistic efficiency and dexterity' and 'equivalence' suggesting the 'preservation of the same meaning'. In this sense, translators, on the one hand, are regarded as manipulators of the target language, in their search for equivalence in order to preserve 'the soul and the essence of the source language'; and traductologists, on the other, are viewed as analysts of the linguistic devices of both the source language and the target language, and as the propounders of theories and models that might offer a good description and a clear explanation of the issues derived from the two languages coming into contact. This task carried out by traductologists should apparently be useful to the translator, and therefore the traductologist's and the translator's jobs ought to tend towards a common point. Unluckily they do not always converge; many translators believe that traductologists are mere theoreticians of language, who are very distant from the true heart of translation. However, it goes without saying that a good knowledge of the nature of language, in the light of different linguistic theories, can be of great use to the translator, and a little experience in translation can do no harm to the speculative traductologist concerned with descriptions, models and theories.

2 Language and Linguistic Paradigms: Structuralism

Linguistic devices, which are, as we have just pointed out, the subject-matter of experts in translemics or traductology, are apparently not universal instruments to all outward appearances, as they are entirely dependent on the prevailing concept of language. As T. Kuhn[5] has pointed out, reality, whether linguistic, artistic or scientific, cannot be examined from a neutral point of view; it is never free of expectations, beliefs or previous experiences: it is always apprehended from the tenets of a theory or of an established point of view, in this case, the prevailing linguistic theory about language.

Heraclitus and Darwin taught us that nothing is static; everything changes and progresses; and, fortunately, linguistic theories are also open to change and advancement. Kuhn has asserted, in his diagnosis of scientific inquiry, that progress in science follows the same patterns as in literature, music, the arts and humanities: stable periods of research within an established scientific framework, characterized by the supremacy of a major theory and by a broad coincidence of scientific goals and methods, are followed by an inevitable generational fracture, which implies the abandonment of apparently well-founded scientific styles and fashions that had been previously the cornerstones of research, and the subsequent appearance of a new preponderant framework.

'Paradigms' is the name given by Thomas Kuhn to these dominant frameworks.[6] For him a paradigm is a consistent scientific structure that provides the scientific community with the necessary theoretical and practical principles for (1) the establishment of new scientific goals and methods, (2) the selection of relevant events that will eventually be turned into research problems, and (3) the proposal of solutions to these problems.

In the second part of the twentieth century, structuralism, generativism and pragmatics have been three of the most outstanding paradigms that have offered a rich and fruitful background to theoretical speculation and applied work in linguistic research. And, although several explanations can be pinpointed as the generators of the fracture causing the change from one paradigm to another, probably 'scientific fatigue', that is, the depletion of intellectual strength accompanied by general dissatisfaction and weariness with current methods and goals, is probably the most powerful reason that might justify the emergence of new paradigms.

The first third of this century was the time when structuralism appeared on both sides of the Atlantic, with the publication of two seminal texts (Saussure's *Cours de Linguistique Générale* and Bloomfield's *Language*), due to the fact that a great many scholars had become tired of the goals and methods of historical linguistics that had overwhelmingly controlled the territory of linguistic research in the 19th century.

Structuralism, with its atomistic and taxonomical approach to language analysis and, to a certain extent, generativism as well, made us aware of many significant and meaningful parts, pieces, sections, portions and segments of language organization, that had not been so transparently presented in the past, and also taught us how all these units and elements are brought together in an orderly arrangement and disposition. Thanks to structuralism, language has been conceived as a well-organized inventory of structures, levels, components and relations, all interlocked in harmonious patterns.

In sum, this atomistic approach has facilitated a deeper understanding of the whole linguistic *system* of the sentence and of its phonological, morphosyntactic, lexical and semantic subsystems; and, at the same time, it has laid the solid foundations for the development of one of the most rewarding fields of linguistics applied to translation: *contrastive analysis*.

This area of research has revealed, in a very transparent way, the most striking differences in the phonological, morphosyntactic, lexical and semantic subsystems of two languages in contact. Although it first applied to language teaching, as it was thought that most problems in language learning emerged from the interference of problematic points, its results have been useful to translation studies.

3 Structuralism and Traductology: Semantic Equivalence

The word 'equivalence' in reference to the tasks and goals of the translator, has been mentioned in the first point, unaccompanied by any qualifier. However, in the midst of the great structuralist boom, 'equivalence' became 'semantic equivalence' when Eugene Nida asserted that the study of *semantic equivalence* was one of the essential prerequisites in order to tackle the problems of translation.[7] Contrastive analysis, and especially *contrastive lexicology*, have doubtless made major contributions to a clearer and more cogent understanding of *semantic equivalence*. And the consequences and contributions of this contrastive lexicology to translation and traductology can be better assessed in the research put into practice in (1) contrastive lexical fields, (2) contrastive synonymy and polysemy, and (3) contrastive deceptive cognates or 'false friends'.

Research in these three branches of contrastive lexicology was not new, as it had been conducted regularly in the past in a more or less intuitive way; the merit of structuralism, however, lay in the fact that it offered a clear and coherent methodology, which stimulated and inspired many research projects.

Thanks to the comparison of *lexical fields*, such as *brillar* (*centellear, refulgir, rielar, titilar,* etc.) in Spanish, and 'shine' (sparkle, gleam, flicker, glow, etc.), in English, we now have clearer and less ambiguous semantic and stylistic contours, both in denotation and connotation, in intension and extension, of the meanings of the specific lexical terms that cluster around the meaning of more general terms.

The work done in lexical *synonymy* by Stephen Ullmann, for example, has been an impressive guide for a better awareness of the connotative meanings of synonyms in a language, like English, that may have equivalent terms from two different origins (Anglo-Saxon and Latin) or even three different origins (Anglo-Saxon, Latin and French). This work can be useful in translating literary texts, for example, the poems of the Irish poet Mahon, who uses Latin-root words in certain circumstances and Anglo-Saxon words in others.

Polysemy has always been a stumbling block and a source of disorienta-
tion for translators, especially because they have often been tempted,
without offering much resistance, to fall into the trap of using unwanted
'calques', which in most cases could have been easily avoided. Polysemies
appear even in specialized areas such as legal English, for example in the
translation into Spanish of the word 'case', which in English has, at least,
four or five different legal meanings. In the Spanish version of the film *JFK*,
on the assassination of President John F. Kennedy, this word is regularly
translated as *caso* in expressions where Spanish has clear-cut terms, which
are much more suitable; in this way, the expression 'the basis/merits of the
case', which in Spanish is *el fondo de la cuestión*, is translated as *la base del
caso*; 'the theory of the case', which in Spanish is *tesis mantenida o expuesta
por cualquiera de las partes*, is translated as *la teoría del caso*; 'You have no
case', which in Spanish is *Carece Vd. de soporte legal* is translated as *Vd. no
tiene caso*, etc. Following Torrents dels Prats,[8] the legal term 'case' has got
very clear counterparts in Spanish: (1), *asunto* as in *Tengo muchos asuntos
pendientes*; (2) *causa, pleito, proceso, litigio, expediente*; (3) *argumentos, razones
que le asisten a uno, fundamentos en que basar una petición, pretensión legítima,
reivindicaciones, justificación, ventajas*; (4) *defensa, acusación, base para la
defensa/acusación, argumentos jurídicos, fundamentos de derecho*, and many
more, including *caso*.

False friends or *deceptive cognates* have also been the origin of many
embarrassing situations.[9] One of those unlucky circumstances arose in 1991
due to a poor translation of the French word *assisté* into English as
'assisted', which was the cause of a certain diplomatic friction between
France and the United States of America.[10] An article about Gerard
Depardieu's disordered childhood explicitly stated that he had 'assisted' a
rape, when from the recorded interview, which was the source of the
article, it was clear that he had 'observed' that criminal act.

The results of contrastive linguistics have been more remarkable in
lexicology but they have also been useful in syntax. For example, the
translation of 'I have been his sole agent since 1932' as *He sido su agente
exclusivo desde 1932* in the statement of claim of a civil action brought by a
sole agent against his principal, instead of *Soy su agente desde 1932*, led the
judge to dismiss the case as he understood that the plaintiff had admitted
having no further links with the defendant.

In sum, although the structural paradigm may be at the moment on the
wane, interest in *contrastive analysis* is not losing force or intensity at all; it
is contrariwise increasing rather than decreasing because it has broadened

its scope of inquisitiveness to the new meaningful parameters that are being opened in the paradigm of pragmatics.

4   A New Paradigm Emerges: Pragmatics

Structuralists deserve a prominent place in the history of applied linguistics for the accurate and, in some cases, clear descriptions of the different levels, structures and components of the many languages they analysed. Generativists also provided us with careful and detailed studies of linguistic systems and, although their approach to linguistic description and explanation was different, they shared two fundamental characteristics of structuralism: (1) the assumption of the sentence as the maximal unit, and (2) the perception of language as a self-contained linguistic system, though, at the same time they disregarded language use and the communicative aspects of language.

However, in the last decades of this century a great number of linguists have started to feel the 'scientific fatigue' mentioned above, mainly caused by the excessive abstraction or formalization of the predominant theories and models. This fatigue, which is a clear signal of the emergence of a new paradigm, pragmatics, is materializing in (1) the abandonment of the underlying models and theories that had been the basis for the research that had been carried out previously, and in (2) their replacement with new theories that tackle language as something dynamic and operative, which has been called 'language in action'. For the holders of these theories, like Austin & Searle's 'speech acts', Grice's 'cooperative principle', Sperber & Wilson's 'relevance'[11] and many others, linguistic analysis is more the exploration of a dynamic 'communicative phenomenon' than the examination of a static 'linguistic system'.

In this way, pragmatics,[12] is following a different path. It attempts to deal with the problems that arise from language in action, that is, from those areas of study called 'parole' and 'performance', passed over by Saussure and Chomsky respectively in their linguistic study. Pragmatics differs from structuralism and generativism in many ways; it is interested in an interdisciplinary approach and in the empirical analysis of linguistic processes, that is, in the study of language use and functions, since what really matters is what has been called 'communicative competence'. This implies a profound methodological and conceptual change that affects the groundwork of linguistic research and, consequently, in dealing with language in action, pragmatics has had to introduce new categories for its linguistic analysis. Probably one of the greatest novelties of 'language in 'action' is the conception of language as *discourse* (or *text*), and the fact that discourse consists of utterances.

4.1 Discourse (or text)

In pragmatics, language is no longer a group of structures or a set of sentences, as in structuralism or generativism. Language is discourse, and although this term can be intuitively understood, it has to be accounted for by means of a descriptive model. There are many models that have attempted to clarify this new linguistic unit called 'discourse'; most of them include, at least, the following features: cohesion, coherence, progressivity, intentionality, closure, and above all, meaning. *Cohesion* refers to the syntactic connection of all the linguistic units of the text. *Coherence* gives semantic stability to the text. *Progressivity* alludes to the constant flow of information that the text provides the receiver with.[13] *Intentionality* accounts for the fact that no text is neutral, impartial or innocent; there are always some linguistic traits or devices that uncover the stand taken by the author of the text: an adverb or adjective placed in a strategic position, a certain thematic organization, any repetition or ellipsis may lead the receiver of the message to infer the position of the author of the passage. *Closure* is concerned with the examination of linguistic devices that guide us in the perception of the text as something closed.

4.2 Textual or pragmatic meaning

Textual meaning is the most characteristic feature of discourse, as meaning by itself has been the central issue of most linguistic theories. There is void or vacuity where there is no meaning, and in this sense, textual or pragmatic meaning is envisaged as an endless source of senses that develop from a text. As all translators know, every message is wrapped up in such a complex of lexical and pragmatic assumptions and presuppositions that the translation of the simplest term, like *snow*, demands the use of an encyclopedia of culture in lieu of a lexicon.[14] Therefore pragmatic meaning is something too complicated to be reduced to the information elicited in the semantic models of structuralism or generativism.

In order to account for this more detailed description of textual or pragmatic meaning, several elaborate models have been forged, most of which contain, at least, these 'meaningful parameters': context, speech act, lexical implication, pragmatic implication, lexical presupposition and pragmatic presupposition.

The term presupposition refers to various facets of the pragmatic meaning of the passage that its writer or sender assumes are previously known to the hearer or receiver; therefore, they have to be established prior to the utterance of the message and must necessarily be true for the message to make sense and to flow normally.

We seldom assert everything we mean in an explicit and unambiguous way, and it seems conceivable that a society where everything was explicitly asserted would be detestable. For example, the utterance *My son-in-law is on a commercial trip to Japan* contains, among others, these presuppositions: 'I have at least one daughter', 'She is married', etc., which must be true and must be known, or assumed, by the receiver of the message if the flow of information is to proceed without difficulty or impediment. But that utterance also contains a few implications, some of which are lexical, i.e. they arise from the lexical meanings of the words of the utterance ('He will be away for a few days') and others are 'pragmatic implications', also called 'implicatures', for example, 'He probably has a top position in his firm', etc., that derive from our knowledge of the social context. The translation of these facets may generate a few problems as we shall discuss later in Point 6.

4.3 Discourse and information: Thematization, repetition and ellipsis

But language in action is still something more. Language contains information that is constantly flowing in different patterns and arrangements. One of these patterns is the tendency towards repetition and ellipsis of linguistic devices in the source language, that are always meaningful, and therefore cannot be passed over without giving them due care and attention in the target language. In my opinion, English sustains lexical repetition much better than Spanish. For example, in the text that follows, the term *insider trading* is repeated four times; the Spanish translation would only use that term once, and would make use of periphrases and anaphoric and cataphoric elements in their place (*la aludida práctica, el mencionado delito, la ya citada conducta*, etc.).

> The SEC has reinforced the *insider trading* restrictions with promulgation of Rule 14e–3 of the SEC, an independent provision prohibiting *insider trading* in connection with tender offers. Congress has further reinforced these trading restrictions by providing the SEC with the power to seek a treble penalty under the *Insider Trading* Sanctions Act of 1984 (ITSA). This legislation empowers the SEC to base enforcement actions on any recognized theory of *insider trading* restriction.

> It was for industrial tribunals *to deal with* deductions and for County Courts *to deal with* failures to pay.

Consequently, the rendering of textual repetitions and ellipsis is also an important issue of pragmatics and translation.

5 Pragmatics and Traductology: Pragmatic Equivalence

In view of this presentation of some of the new principles of the paradigm of pragmatics, it seems safe to conclude that a new frontier is opening up for translemics and traductology. The first challenge that the traductologist faces in this new frontier, in which 'language is in action', is that *semantic equivalence*, which in the earlier paradigms necessarily dealt with structures, levels and components of the linguistic system, is now broadening its scope to become something more complex and aspiring, called *textual or pragmatic equivalence*. However, the term 'textual', has already been used in previous paradigms, for example, in *Translation Studies*,[15] Bassnett alludes to 'the syntagmatic equivalence of a text, i.e. equivalence of form and shape'.

It is clear that *pragmatic equivalence* has a much wider scope of application than *semantic equivalence*. It includes not only the analysis and comparison of the textual meaning of the same passage written in two different languages, but of all the other textual categories (cohesion, thematization, etc.) that may affect their final perception by the receivers of the two languages, in the light of the theories and models of pragmatics.

Vázquez Ayora distinguishes two main techniques in indirect or oblique translation: transposition and modulation. Transposition is the substitution of a grammatical category of the original message by a different grammatical category of the target language. For example, if the English expression 'He held that . . .', whose nucleus is a verb, is translated into Spanish as *en su opinión*, whose nucleus is a noun, we have performed a transposition of verb to noun; if the expression 'for late delivery' is translated as *demora en la entrega*, there has evidently been a transposition of the adjective 'late' into the substantive *demora*.

Modulation, however, occurs in more abstract categories, the so-called 'categories of thought'; for example, in the translation of 'the keels' for *los barcos* there has been a modulation of the part for the whole. In his *Introducción a la Traductología*, Vázquez Ayora gives an abundant account of the many modulations that can be performed with the 'categories of thought'. In the text that follows we find in (2) a skilful sample of transposition when the noun 'restoration' is translated by the adjective *restaurado*, and a more resourceful case of modulation in (3), when the verb 'demonstrate' (protest outwardly in the street), is translated by one of its semantic parts or components (*la calle*):

Puerto Rico's linguistic schizophrenia is not a consequence of last Thursday's (1) restoration (2) of equal legal status for both Spanish and English, although the new law prompted thousands of citizens to demonstrate (3) repeatedly against a decision they considered unfair. It was born of the difficult coexistence with English, the language of the ruling nation. And also, on the mainland, of the growth of a fascinating and controversial hybrid: Spanglish. On the island, demonstrators called for a return to 'the Spanish of Puerto Rico not of Spain.'

La esquizofrenia lingüística que padece Puerto Rico no nace de (1) la co-oficialidad, restaurada (2) el jueves, del español y del inglés, aunque esta ley ha volcado a la calle (3), y varias veces, a millares de ciudadanos que consideran injusta la decisión. Nace de una historia de difícil coexistencia con el inglés de la potencia administradora. Y también, en el continente, del crecimiento de un apasionante y polémico híbrido, el «Spanglish». En la isla, el español reivindicado en la calle no es «el de España, queremos hablar el español de Puerto Rico».   El Mundo, 30 January 1993

At this stage I would like to claim that (1) semantic equivalence is the goal of transposition and that pragmatic equivalence is the goal of modulation, and that (2) the mastery of both techniques is indispensable to the professional translator. In my opinion, the translator of the passage from Aldous Huxley's *Point Counter Point* that follows was not very successful in the transposition and modulation of the underlined expressions, which sound forced or unnatural in Spanish, especially the qualification of the adjectives *frívolo, serio y adulto*. The native speaker of Spanish would think of other more 'natural' expressions, like *Yo no soy ni tan listo ni tan frívolo, etc.*, instead of the forced expression *tan completa y purilmente frívolo*:

— *Yo no soy* tan completa y puerilmente frívolo *como pareces figurarte* tú – *dijo con dignidad y cólera contenida.*

— *Al contrario – contestó ella – eres* demasiado adultamente serio. *Serías incapaz de ocuparte de un niño, porque no eres bastante niño tú mismo. Tú eres como uno de esos personajes* espantosamente adultos *de la* Matusalén *de Bernard Shaw.*

Aldous Huxley, *Point Counter Point* (Harmondsworth: Penguin, 1955); trans. Lino Novas, *Contrapunto* (Buenos Aires: Edhasa, 1978). p. 403

'I'm not *quite so childishly frivolous* as you seem to imagine,' he said with dignity and bottled anger.

'On the contrary,' she answered, 'you're *too adultly serious*. You couldn't manage a child because you're not enough of a child yourself. You're like one of those *dreadfully grown-up. creatures* in Shaw's *Methuselah*.' (p. 312).

6 Pragmatic Meaning and the Polyphony of the Literary Text

As we have said in 4.2, we seldom assert explicitly everything we mean, and it is easily understood that a social community that called for all the messages to be categorically expressed would be hardly bearable. However, this feature of language is at times disadvantageous for translation, since the message may run the risk of not being understood, much less enjoyed, if it is a literary text, when a great number of the presuppositions and implications conveyed in the passage are lost or misinterpreted.

As the conveying of lexical and pragmatic presuppositions and implicatures is certainly one of the weakest points of translation, and of traductology, a few proposals have been put forward to find a suitable answer to this problem. Blakemore, for example, assigns a great importance to context and, consequently, suggests forging similar contexts that might yield the same interpretation of the utterance of a writer or speaker.

Some classical literary texts provide the readers with the 'pragmatic presupposition' that they must be aware of from the very beginning of the story; for example, Jane Austen's 'It's a truth universally acknowledged that a single man in possession of a large fortune must be in want of a wife' from *Pride and Prejudice* is an important pragmatic presupposition that the narrator has included in the text to guide the reader.

However, most texts are not so explicit and they do not often provide the reader with pragmatic presuppositions or with pragmatic implications. Leo Hickey[16] claims that in order to avoid 'distorting the stylistic effect' there could be a 'middle course'. Following his suggestion, the translator is led to manipulate, especially by resorting to the use of the technique of modulation, some of the 'voices' of the text, especially the voice of the omniscient narrator, and of the authorial and the intrusive narrators as well, or even the voices of the characters, in order to introduce the word or the words that would prevent the reader from losing indispensable presuppositions or implications. The translator is entitled to insert these slight changes, always through the constant use of the technique of modulation, because the voice of the narrator has two main functions: (1) to be an alert and knowledgeable *filter* of all the events and circumstances that take place in the story, and (2) to create a degree of *attachment to* or sympathy with towards the characters. This last feature of attachment can be easily lost when presuppositions and implications cannot be properly inferred in the target language.

7 Cohesion, Coherence, Presupposition and Implication in Pragmatic Equivalence

There are many more significant paths and categories that pragmatics offers as a new basis for the development of new lines of research, including thematization, cohesion in translation, and coherence in translation.

7.1 The information flow: Thematization

One of the goals of translators, as was stated above, is the preservation of the essence of the source language in the text of the target language. Bearing this point in mind, translators immediately face a troublesome choice: are they obliged to respect the 'discourse orientation' of the original text, i.e. its thematic order, or are they allowed to manipulate this order in pursuing their attempt to preserve the 'essence of the message'?

This issue of thematization, which is certainly very significant, arises most frequently in the translation of legal texts. For example, the following sentence has different thematic orientations in English and in Spanish:

> Persons bringing a derelict ship or goods belonging to her, into port, raising a sunken ship, securing wreck, or protecting the cargo of a stranded vessel by transshipping it, or removing it to a place of safety, *may be entitled to salvage.*

> Pueden reclamar la indemnización por el servicio de salvamento *quienes lleven a puerto,* etc.

And the passage that follows can have, at least, four different thematizations in Spanish:

> A prospective tenant who pays quarterly rent for possession of premises pending negotiation of the lease is not presumed to have acquired a quarterly tenancy.

In the first version the nucleus of the verbal predicate (*is not presumed*) has been thematized:

> *No debe presumirse que necesariamente adquiere la condición de inquilino periódico el que durante la fase de negociaciones del arrendamiento pague una renta trimestral por el alquiler de un local.*

In this second version the theme is a complement of the subject (*el hecho de que . . . pague*):

El hecho de que un inquilino potencial que durante la fase de negociaciones del arrendamiento pague una renta trimestral por el alquiler de un local, no ha entenderse necesariamente como que adquiere la condición de inquilino periodico o trimestral.

This third version follows more closely the thematic organization of the English text:

El inquilino potencial, que durante la fase de negociaciones del arrendamiento, pague una renta trimestral por el alquiler de un local, no adquiere necesariamente la condición de inquilino de régimen periódico o trimestral.

This last version is similar to the previous one but resorts to a generalization in the plural (*Quienes siendo . . .*):

Quienes siendo inquilinos potenciales paguen una renta trimestral por el alquiler de un local durante la fase de negociaciones de su arrendamiento, no adquieren necesariamente la condición de inquilinos de régimen periódico o trimestral.

7.2 Cohesion in translation

Cohesion in translation is magnificently illustrated by Dámaso Alonso's rendering of James Joyce's *A Portrait of the Artist as a Young Man*,[17] especially in the use of the deictic pronouns *éste* y *ésta* in 'Éste era el cuento . . .' y 'Ésta era la canción . . .':

Once upon a time and a very good time it was there was a moocow coming down along the road and this moocow that was coming down along the road met a nicens little boy named baby tuckoo . . ..

His father told him that story: his father looked at him through a glass: he had a hairy face.

He was a baby tuckoo. The moocow came down the road where Betty Byrne lived: she sold lemon platt.

> O, the wild rose blossoms
> On the little green place.

He sang that song. That was his song.

Allá en otros tiempos (y bien buenos tiempos que eran), había una vez una vaquita (¡mu!) que iba por un caminito. Y esa vaquita que iba por un caminito se encontró un niñín muy guapín, al cual le llamaban el nene de la casa . . .

Éste era el cuento que contaba su padre. Su padre le miraba a través de un cristal; tenía la cara peluda.

El era el nene de la casa. La vaquita venía por el caminito donde vivía Betty Byrne: Betty Byrne vendía trenzas de azúcar al limón.

Ay, las flores de las rosas silvestres
en el pradecito verde.

Ésta *era la canción que cantaba. Era su canción*

The Spanish rendering of this passage works for several reasons:

(1) The parallelistic syntactic repetition (*Éste era el cuento que contaba su padre/Ésta es la canción que cantaba*) achieved in the Spanish version probably has a greater poetic rhythm than its English counterpart ('His father told him that story' and 'He sang that song. That was his song').

(2) The use of the deictic *éste* and *ésta* in Spanish, which has not been magnetized by the mere mechanical reproduction of the English 'that', is more significant in Spanish than in English, as it has two clear functions: in the first place, it connects what follows with the preceding information and, in the second place, it alerts readers to the emergence of a new topic, in this case, a commentary about the tale and the song.

(3) The repetition of the voiceless velar stops in *cantaba, contaba, cuento, canción* helps to create a subliminal rhythmic effect, which is similar to that accomplished in the original version through the repetition of 'song, sang, song'.

These 'conscious' repetitions are of great value and deserve the reader's gratitude, because they are not only meaningful but cooperate, at the same time, in the construction of the cohesion of the text, as we can see in the original version of Buero Vallejo's *En la ardiente oscuridad*:[18]

Andrés	Hace un rato *que dieron las diez y media.*
Pedro	*Y la apertura del curso es a las once.*
Elisa	*Yo os preguntaba si habían dado ya los tres cuartos.*
Lolita	*Hace un rato que nos lo has preguntado por tercera vez.*

Andrés	You heard the clock strike ten-thirty a moment ago.
Pedro	And we don't have to be at the opening ceremony until eleven.
Elisa	I was only asking if you'd heard it strike a quarter of eleven.
Lolita	It's only the third time you've asked.

The author has repeated *hace un rato* twice in thematic position (*Hace un rato que dieron las diez y media. Hace un rato que nos lo has preguntado por tercera vez*), but probably the translator of the English version seems not to be aware of the value of this thematic repetition or else disregarded it as being an 'unwanted' repetition. However, to be fair, the special effect of this repetition is not lost in the English version; by means of a modulation with the use of 'it's only', the connotation of insistence becomes a hint of irony or sarcasm in English with 'It's only the third time you've asked'.

7.3 Coherence in translation

This is also achieved in Dámaso Alonso's translation of James Joyce's *A Portrait of the Artist as a Young Man*. In the passage that follows, James Joyce makes use of *he*. However, Dámaso Alonso resorts to *Stephen* in both cases. The translator probably thinks that the name to which *he* alludes has been left far behind in the text, and in order not to lose the thread of the story he uses *Stephen*; in the second case, as the appearance of another proper name, Lawton, may be negative for the coherence of the text, the translator resorts to *Stephen* again in order to avoid any misunderstanding.

> *He* kept on the fringe of his line, out of sight of his prefect, out of the reach of the rude feet, feigning to run now and kicking and stamping. Then Jack Lawton's yellow boots dodged out the ball and the other boots and legs ran after. *He* ran after them a little way and then stopped. It was useless to run on.

> Stephen *se mantenía en el extremo de su línea, fuera de la vista del prefecto, fuera del alcance de piernas y puntapiés. De pronto las botas amarillas de Lawton lanzaron el balón fuera del corro y todas las otras botas y piernas corrieron detrás.* Stephen *corrió también un trecho y luego se paró. No tenía objeto el seguir.*

However, when the translator does not modulate because he is too concerned to follow the syntax of the original text, the result can be tiring, and the excess of anaphoric markers (*él, ella*), can be counterproductive, as we have empirically tested in the passage that follows. In this case, ellipsis could have turned out more fruitful for the preservation of the original coherence:

> Realizing her power, Gladys began to withhold what he desired. Perhaps he could be blackmailed into the generosity which it was not in his nature to display spontaneously. Returning from a very inexpensive evening at Lyon's and the pictures, she pushed him angrily away when, in the taxi, he attempted the usual endearments.

> 'Can't you leave me in peace?' she snapped. And a moment later, 'Tell the driver to go to my place first and drop me.'

> 'But my dyah child!' Mr Quarles protested. Hadn't she promised to come back with him? (p. 310).

> *Dándose cuenta de su poder, Gladys comenzó a rehusar aquello que deseaba* él. *Acaso fuera posible forzarlo por medio del chantaje a desplegar una generosidad que no estaba en su naturaleza desplegar espontáneamente. Al regreso de una noche muy poco onerosa en la casa de comidas y en el*

cinematógrafo, ella *le rechazó, colérica, cuando, en el taxi, trató* él *de prodigarle las caricias acostumbradas.*

— *¿No puede dejarme en paz?* – *dijo secamente.* Y *un momento después: Dígale al chófer que nos lleve primero a mi casa para apearme.*

— *Pero, ¡cielito mío, venga usted acá!* – *protestó Quarles.* ¿*No le había prometido* ella *regresar con él?* (p. 400).

See also the unnecessary and tiring repetitions of *yo* and *tú* in the passage by the same author that starts with *Yo no soy* tan completa y puerilmente frívolo *como pareces.* In addition, the translation of 'withold' as *rehusar,* and of 'display' as *desplegar* are not very productive; *negarle* and *mostrar* would have been more natural.

8 Conclusion

This paper has acknowledged the important contributions of the models which emerged from structuralism and generativism in the earlier stages of linguistic analysis applied to translation, but claims that new and more profound potentialities for a better understanding of the act of translation and of traductology may be found within the theories and models offered by the new linguistic paradigm called pragmatics: the analysis and contrast of the textual meanings (implication, presupposition, etc.) of the passages of the source and the target languages, and the examination of their textual features, such as cohesion, coherence, thematization, etc. will, in all likelihood, widen the scope of translation studies.

Notes

1. Cf. Gerardo Vázquez Ayora, *Introducción a la traductología* (Washington DC: Georgetown University Press, 1977); Julio César Santoyo and Rosa Rabadán, 'Traductología/translémica. *Una nueva disciplina lingüística', Revista española de lingüística aplicada* (Granada: AESLA, 1990); and G. Radó, 'Outline of a Systematic Translatology. The Terminology of Translation', *Meta,* 30, 4 (1985), pp. 34–52.
2. W. Wills, *The Science of Translation* (Tubingen: Gunter Narr Verlag, 1982); and Lauren Leighton *The Art of Translation* (Knoxville: The University of Tennessee Press, 1984).
3. Philip Lewis, 'The measure of translation effects' in Joseph F. Graham (ed.), *Difference in Translation* (Ithaca and London: Cornell University Press, 1985).
4. William Frawley, 'Prolegomenon to a Theory of Translation', in William Frawley, ed, *Translation. Literary, Linguistic and Philosophic Perspectives* (London and Toronto: Associated University Presses, 1979), pp. 159–74.
5. Thomas Kuhn, *The Structure of Scientific Revolutions* (Chicago: The University of Chicago Press, 1962) and *The Essential Tension* (Chicago: The University of Chicago Press, 1977).

6. Enrique Alcaraz, *Tres paradigmas de la investigación lingüística* (Alcoy: Marfil, 1990).
7. Eugene Nida, *Language Structure and Translation* (Stanford: Stanford University Press, 1975).
8. A. Torrents dels Prats, *Diccionario de dificultades del inglés* (Barcelona: Juventud, 1976), pp. 70–2.
9. R. J. Hill, *A Dictionary of False Friends*. (London: McMillan, 1982).
10. Victor de la Serna en 'Traduttore, traditore', *El Mundo*, 6.4.1991, p. C4.
11. J. L. Austin, *How to Do Things with Words* (London: Clarendon Press, 1962); J. R. Searle *et al.*, *Speech Acts, Theory and Pragmatics* (Dordrecht: Reidel, 1980); H. P. Grice, 'Logic and conversation', pp. 44–58 in Cole, P. and J. L. Morgan, eds., *Syntax and Semantics, Vol. 3: Speech Acts*. (New York: Academic Press, 1975); D. Sperber and D. Wilson, 'Mutual Knowledge and Relevance in Theories of Comprehension', pp. 61–85 in N. V. Smith (ed.), *Relevance: Communication and Cognition*. (London: Blackwell, 1986).
12. Charles Morris, *Signs, Language and Behavior* (New York: Prentice Hall, 1946).
13. O. Ducrot, *Decir y no decir* (Barcelona: Anagrama, 1982).
14. Frawley, *art. cit.*, p. 159.
15. Susan Bassnett, *Translation Studies* (London: Routledge, 1991).
16. Leo Hickey *et al.*, 'A Pragmastylistic Aspect of Literary Translation', *Babel*, 39, 2 (1993), pp. 77–88.
17. James Joyce, *A Portrait of the Artist as Young Man* (St. Albans: Triad/Panther Books, 1977); trans. Dámaso Alonso, *El artista adolescente* (Madrid: Alianza, 1978).
18. Antonio Buero Vallejo, *En la ardiente oscuridad* (Madrid: Espasa Calpe, 1972); trans. Marion Peter Holt, *In the Burning Darkness* (New York: Trinity University Press, 1985).

7 Translation, Counter-Culture, and *The Fifties* in the USA

EDWIN GENTZLER

> *In this country we have two streams of culture. We have a commercial culture, of Saul Bellow and the* Saturday Review *and all of that, and underneath there is another culture, not really touched upon by the upper stream.*
>
> Robert Bly, *Talking All Morning*

Introduction

In this paper I intend to (1) express concern over recent developments in the 'theory' branch of translation studies, i.e., the attempt to formulate 'laws' regarding translation phenomena based upon little supportive evidence; (2) offer an alternative approach to thinking about literary systems, one that takes into account the complex functioning of literary translations in any given culture; and (3) illustrate this approach by looking at the 'use' of literary translation in the journal *The Fifties*, edited by Robert Bly and William Duffy.[1] The problem may reside in the polysystem hypothesis regarding the role of translations in 'strong' cultures. Scholars such as Itamar Even-Zohar and Gideon Toury[2] argue that literary translations use norms and stylistic conventions which are often 'secondary', 'out of date', 'common', and 'remote from centers of innovation'. I will address hypotheses formulated by Itamar Even-Zohar in 'Universals of Literary Contacts' (*Papers on Historical Poetics*, 1978), specifically, that translated texts tend to behave like a secondary system with respect to source language texts (No. 11); that translated texts tend to appropriate from established source language texts genres (No. 12); and that this appropriation tends to be simplified, regularized and schematized (No.

13). Even-Zohar writes, for example, 'It is relatively established that what I would call "secondary activities" (translation, non-canonized literature, epigonic literature) tend to regularize patterns which are relatively free in a given source (a source text [for translation], canonized literature [for non-canonized], major literature [for epigonic]'.[3] While Even-Zohar observes that translations can function as primary or innovative in 'young' literatures or in systems which are 'weak', he seldom observes such functioning in 'strong' literary systems; the only time Even-Zohar allows for translations to occupy a primary position in such a literature is when that culture is in 'crisis'.[4] While Even-Zohar does recognize a paradox in his formulations, i.e. that translations even in strong cultures do introduce new ideas and literary devices into a system, he nevertheless maintains that they are used as 'a means to preserve traditional taste'.[5] I find Even-Zohar's analysis of translations in well-developed literary systems highly formalistic and essentialist, invariably assuming the perspective of the literary centre itself.

I would like to suggest that translation studies consider another model of systems theory, one that assumes the perspective of those peripheral minority groups far from the centre of literary innovation. In the second section of this paper I will briefly sketch how I think Michel de Certeau's form of thinking, in both *The Practice of Everyday Life* (translated by Steven Rendell, 1984) and *Heterologies: Discourse on the Other* (translated by Brian Massumi, 1986) might be useful to translation studies scholars whose corpora do not fit into the existing polysystem model. Finally, I look at the way literary translations were used by Robert Bly in his journal *The Fifties*, focusing primarily on translations of Spanish poets Juan Ramón Jiménez (1881–1936), Antonio Machado (1875–1939), and Federico García Lorca (1898–1936). The thesis I am exploring here is that literary translations, rather than resulting from a cultural crisis, as hypothesized by ps-theory, may play an important role in *causing* that crisis. In Bly's case, the translated material did not conform to existing norms, but was highly original and in turn instrumental in changing the literary and cultural centres in the United States.

Polysystem Theory

Polysystem theory was developed in articles written during the early 1970s by Itamar Even-Zohar and collected in *Papers in Historical Poetics* (1978). The term 'polysystem' represents the aggregate of literary systems, including everything from 'high' forms such as innovative verse to 'low' forms such as romance novels and children's literature. Even-Zohar recognized both the 'primary', i.e. creating new genres and styles, and 'secondary', i.e. reinforcing existing genres and styles, function of translation within the polysystem. He also divided his thinking about the role translations play in the polysystem along two lines, noting that (1) in cultures that are 'weak' translations tend to play a strong or primary role and are located in the literary centre; and (2) in cultures that are 'strong' translations tend to play a secondary role and tend to be marginalized by the literary centres.

The data coming in from case studies all over the world seems to support Even-Zohar's claims regarding the former situation. Polysystem theory, as a tool for studying the literatures from emerging nations, from developing countries, or countries undergoing radical change, is becoming increasingly indispensable. With regard to Israel, the central importance of literary translations to the development of the culture of post-war Israeli society should come as no surprise, given its unusual position as a mandated nation state with no previously existing literary centres or institutions, nor its own contemporary literature or literary models. Equally interesting, however, are the results of case studies from earlier periods – translations in nineteenth-century Czech culture, translations in England during the fifteenth century, and translations into Latin American cultures during their formative stages.

What makes the polysystem hypothesis so exciting is that once you have grasped it, you can see the process unfold before your very eyes. In Canada's recent election, for example, the Bloc Québècois experienced enormous success, winning 54 seats to emerge as the most powerful opposition party. One could argue that two nations currently exist within one, and the new nation is about to emerge. Certainly the possibility of Quebec independence is a serious one. The role translations have played in forming identities and subverting established institutions has been well-documented by a group of feminist translation scholars in Montreal and Quebec. Some would argue that theatre translations, more than anything else, contributed to this process of cultural differentiation. In a prophetic 1989 article, Annie Brisset talks about questions of translation, politics, and national identity in 'In Search of a Target Language: The Politics of Theatre Translation in Quebec'. Translation is seen as a symbolic act of autonomy, a fulfilling of a desire for a language of one's own. Translation, or often in the case of Quebec, retranslation (as many of the texts have already been translated into French), was an important way of articulating one's own vocabulary, one's own way of thinking, which, in the Quebec case, was far removed from the French of France. Translation, according to scholars like Brisset,[6] is less a way of introducing a foreign text and more a way of legitimizing a distinct ethnological and political entity, in this case Quebec itself.

Less convincing are Even-Zohar's arguments concerning the opposite condition, i.e. the role of translations in 'strong' cultures such as the French, British, or Russian, with well-developed literary traditions and many different kinds of writing. Even-Zohar maintains that in such situations, only 'original' writing produces innovations in ideas and forms, and that translation recedes in importance. He makes statements such as 'no literary structures on any level were ever adopted by the non-canonized system before they had become common stock of the canonized one',[7] that 'translated literature in this case becomes a major factor in conservatism',[8] and that 'while the contemporary literature might go on developing new norms and models, translated literature adheres to norms which have either been recently or long before rejected by the (newly) established center'.[9] Here my objections multiply. First of all, I am not sure the data support his thesis. More importantly, I find his concept of 'original' loaded with aesthetic and ideological preconceptions, especially in the literary hierarchies he establishes, with poetic verse at the top and 'lesser' forms of original writing, such as detective fiction, at the bottom. I would argue with any 'trickle-down' model which presupposes that elements originating in high literary material naturally descend into popular writing, and eventually into the extra-literary. Finally, I would dispute Even-Zohar's claim that translations in strong nations invariably assume forms already established within a particular genre and conform to norms which the 'higher' forms have already rejected. If indeed translation seems so crucial to cultural formation in emerging nations, might not the same postulate apply to all cultures, weak or strong?

I find it unfortunate that Even-Zohar's formulations, hastily and often provocatively developed during the seventies, have exerted such enormous influence on subsequent scholarship. Gideon Toury, for example, in a 1991 essay 'What are Descriptive Studies into Translation Likely to Yield apart from Isolated Descriptions' in *Translation Studies: The State of the Art* (1991) makes similar claims. He writes, 'We seem to have hit on the ultimate goal of translation studies now: the formulation of a coherent set of LAWS OF TRANSLATION BEHAVIOUR of the form 'if X, then the greater/the smaller the likelihood of Y',[10] and then cites one example, which 'current research has been able to come up with'. The law reads as follows: 'In translation, extremes tend to be converted to repertoremes'. Toury translates this single law into a variety of increasingly less jargon-laden vocabularies to end with the following claim: 'translation tends to assume a *peripheral* position in the target system, generally employing *secondary* models and serving as a major factor of *conservatism'*. Here is the same 'trickle-down' thesis characteristic of 'strong' nations that Even-Zohar generated as a hypothesis in 1978, now taking the form of a 'law' backed by research data carried out in the eighties. According to Toury, 'Descriptive research has amply demonstrated that it is seldom broken'.[11] After a decade of research, has translation studies learned nothing new? Does descriptive research simply validate the provisional hypothesis with which it began? According to Toury, the evolution of theory in the field seems merely to confirm a model of systemic behaviour derived in the seventies *before* anyone looked at the real conditions of production. In this particular essay, Toury documents his findings with just one example of such research, an MA thesis in Tel Aviv. Is not something missing? What precisely might these laws and this rhetoric conceal? In my opinion, the discourse in which these laws are formulated – and the assumption of consensus among translation scholars who have already been trained to use Toury's model – may close down or limit alternative interpretations of the same data. By assuming a centrist position within such cultures, the translation scholar may in fact perpetuate certain stereotypes about translation, reconfirming its marginal status. Is the ultimate purpose of translation theory to generate laws in the first place?

In fact, many case studies indicate that translations can be used as a cultural weapon in a struggle to break down the norms of an established system. For example, one could hardly call England early in the twentieth century a 'weak' nation. Yet Ezra Pound was able to introduce multiple new forms, such as Anglo-Saxon alliterative verse or the Japanese *haiku*, into the literary system via translation. Recent scholarship in the British literary system seems to indicate that *all* important changes in poetics over the last 500 years were led not by 'original' writing in the Toury/Even-Zohar sense, but via translations. Perhaps we need to rethink the vocabulary of 'weak' and 'strong' cultures altogether. Many African literary systems, for example, are oral in nature, perhaps some of the oldest and strongest oral traditions in the world; would a ps-theorist call the African system weak? Likewise, what is 'original writing'? Many African 'literary' texts tend to be (1) already translations from another language and (2) translations that are already rewritings of *performances* or several performances, duly smoothed out and shaped to conform to the limitations of the language (often French or English) in which they are being packaged. Just what is the 'original text' in this case? Clearly the oral form. Which system is 'weak'? Perhaps the western language. Which system is strong? Perhaps the marginalized system. In such a situation, is it useful to use terms like 'strong' or 'weak' at all? Is ps-theory biased in favor of written forms? Various powerful and culturally rich processes were clearly already involved in the generation of many 'original' texts. What are the differences in the two traditions? To what extent do the terminology, and the cultural perspective with which we analyze such differences, determine what we see?

Toury and Even-Zohar would no doubt argue that all African nations are 'weak' and therefore not relevant as a challenge to previous analyses of the role of translations in nations with strong literary systems. Although the classification is loaded with socio-political implications, for the purpose of this discussion, let us accept the ps-terms and focus on a 'strong' nation: post-World War II USA. In the 1950s, the US was one of two world super-powers militarily, enjoyed a rich and diversified literary system, one that spanned the spectrum of traditional, popular, political, and highly experimental forms of writing. The period is generally perceived as politically stable and socially conservative; Dwight D. Eisenhower was president, Richard Nixon vice-president. Compared to earlier decades, the general population enjoyed economic prosperity and a high employment rate. MacDonalds mass produced hamburgers, General Motors mass produced autos and developers like those at Levittown mass produced homes. Industrial success stories fuelled a higher standard of living and the perception of general prosperity. The corpus I chose to examine includes poetry translations in the USA during the fifties and early sixties, concentrating on Bly's translations from Spanish. My initial data seem to show that translation, rather than being a conservative force, rather than conforming to already existing models and normative behaviour, actually preceded and spear-headed the search by the new generation, a decade later, for alternative models of expression.

Michel De Certeau

Before looking at the state of literary translation in the USA during the 1950s, I would like to interject another model for translation/cultural studies, based less on Formalist and more on continental philosophy. The two texts central to my current thinking on this subject are Michel de Certeau's *The Practice of Everyday Life*, translated by Steven Rendell (1984) and *Heterologies: Discourse on the Other*, translated by Brian Massumi (1986).

De Certeau has written about theology or the history of religion, about anthropology, about how histories are constructed, about contemporary cultural criticism, literary theory, and about cooking. He taught, up until his recent death, in Los Angeles and Paris. I see De Certeau's work in a continuing intertextual line that begins with Nietzsche, continues through

Heidegger, and Derrida. Yet as Nietzsche, Heidegger and Derrida seem preoccupied with the philosophical question of the nature of being, De Certeau focuses on questions regarding smaller, seemingly less important, almost mundane aspects of language. Whereas Nietzsche, Heidegger and Derrida employ difficult concepts such as 'beyond good and evil' (Nietzsche), 'pre-ontic-ontological thinking' (Heidegger), or *différance* (Derrida) to reveal or at least to approach 'the other', De Certeau uses popular culture to reach a similar location.

De Certeau's definition of popular culture revolves less around static notions of what or who the masses are, and more around what they *do*; he is more interested in daily *practices* than *Dasein*. According to De Certeau, everyday life consists of actions such as shopping, cooking, working, talking, reading, and desiring. While all of the actions that constitute our quotidian existence are of course different, De Certeau organizes his thinking around how people *use* products in their activity, or use representations of products (e.g. in reading, use the text). While Coca-Cola may in fact appear successful at colonizing our brains, reducing us to unreflective, passive consumers, to the extent that some of us subjectively identify with particular products, De Certeau argues that people ordinarily exercise *more* control than theorists may have us believe. For example, the consumer may wait to buy that Coca-Cola until it goes on sale, may buy another brand, may protest the introduction of 'improvements', or may boycott the multi-nationals entirely. In short, consumers have opinions that they do (albeit often unconsciously or spontaneously) exercise.

Theorists such as Toury and Even-Zohar would argue in an abstract fashion that texts get chosen for translation because of certain formal or stylistic 'vacuums' that exist in the target literary system. If, for example, a literature has no detective novels, an Anglo-American or French form might be selected and imported in the same way that air rushes in to fill vacuums in space. Using a quasi-scientific discourse, replete with analogies from physics, the human decision-making process is almost excised from this analysis. Indeed, most systemic or structuralist methodologies fail at the task of linking human agency to historical change. I would suggest, however, that many translators are far less determined by conservative literary nodels than the theory assumes, i.e. that they consciously select the texts they wish to translate because they want to *use* translations to affect certain changes in a culture.

De Certeau uses terms such as 'consumer' to talk about everyday life, but not without pointing out how much is concealed by the very term. 'Consumer' implies a passive, docile, dominated entity, but De Certeau points out that consumers are also makers, users, inventors; he even invokes the Greek term *poiesis*[12] to refer to this 'making' or 'doing' activity of the consumer. Yet poets, novelists, literary critics, film makers, journalists, advertisers, all those active in the production of 'culture', have appropriated the term 'production', leaving no *space* for consumers. Likewise, translation scholars have relegated literary translators to a secondary activity implying that their production is a derivative, dominated kind of activity. De Certeau's model allows us to explore the *poiesis* on the part of the user/translator, that which is often hidden, silent, invisible, but according to De Certeau, insinuated everywhere.

While many sociologists and system theorists have attempted to generate totalizing models that describe and incorporate consumers (the extra-literary) into their systems and explain their behaviour, such generalizations and universalizing claims tend to conceal and cover-up multiple differentiating activities. In fact, De Certeau would go so far as to argue that the practices of everyday life do not conform to any laws of any coherent system. Everyday practices depend upon systems, but are always relative to situations, invariably concealed in those modes of usage which, some scientists and post-structuralist critics argue, constitute them. One metaphor De Certeau invokes to illustrate such phenomena is the 'parasitic' nature of such actions, as in micro-organisms that invade and dwell in the body, yet are able to avoid the body's defense systems as well as the scrutiny of doctors. The system or the state/nation/culture is likened to an invaded and manipulated organism. The practice of everyday life is thus the practice of evasive conformity by which processes of disruption are so small that they cannot be publicly controlled, let alone eliminated, cleansed, or purged. These activities often get termed mundane, secondary or derivative by cultural and literary critics, but they can be very creative. The working mother, for example, is one of the unsung heroes of the twentieth century. What she allows her kids to watch on TV, how she shops, how she stretches her equal pay, what comprises her relationship toward her employer, her very definition of work/pleasure, what she reads and how she reads, what she *does* and how she *does* it, has to, out of necessity, be highly creative. Her behaviour, and the countless different ways in which she uses, makes, invents, and 'makes do', is closely related to De Certeau's definition of the creative nature of the consumer. In fact, De Certeau is perhaps most interested in those surreptitious activities that show the makeshift creativity of individuals trapped or repressed by the system. He is also very interested in unspoken, intuitive, impulsive practices which silently, invisibly disrupt.

Herein lies the connection between De Certeau's project and those of his deconstructionist predecessors. Such invisible actions are invariably *indeterminate*, often unconscious operations; as soon as any procedure becomes established, regularized, normative, such practices change and move on, or 'wander' in De Certeau's terminology. Such actions are defined not by reason or force, but in the evasion of those very systems of reason and force. In De Certeau's words, while users/consumers are governed by language, culture, and systems, their actions also 'trace out the ruses of other interests and desires that are neither determined nor captured by the systems in which they develop'.[13] Their tactics are complex and heterogeneous (thus *Heterologies*),[14] hidden within culture in its customs and normative behaviour. The consumer is thus redefined as an unrecognized producer. Everyday people are viewed as poets (makers) of their own acts. While studies, surveys, statistical investigations may grasp certain elements used, such sociological work does not grasp the artisan-like inventiveness of how elements are combined. The statisticians tend to reorganize the results according to their own codes and, through such organization, lose sight of what they claim to seek and represent. I suggest it is time to recognize literary translators as producers as well, as makers of their own acts and texts.

De Certeau illustrates his work with many examples from shopping, cooking, and reading. He also cites texts, such as the *Art of War* by Chinese author Sun Tzu, and the Arabic anthology *The Book of Tricks*, which helps locate his work. One of the best examples concerns native American Indian cultures, especially the use of Spanish culture by the native American tribes of South America. While becoming on the outside submissive subjects to the *conquistadores*, these native Americans used the rituals, representations and laws of the Spanish for their own purposes. They did not reject them or change them (they had no choice in that matter); indeed they seemed to consent to their own subjugation. Instead, they subverted and redirected them (when they had the choice), *using* them towards ends and references foreign to the dominating system. Think, for example, of the ends to which the Christian religion has been put, or even more specifically, the ends to which the Virgin Mary has been used within Latin America. Within their weakness, the native Americans also exercised power. De Certeau talks in terms of everyday people escaping the dominant social order without leaving it, of how the apparently weak, submissive, subjugated also can and do exercise power. This example of the native American Indian, according to De Certeau, is analogous to any number of contemporary consumers who use the culture shaped by the elites (in, for example, producing language) for their own purposes.[15]

Another example I find illuminating is De Certeau's reading of '*la perruque*', or 'the wig', a term used in France, for example, by workers in a Renault plant, one that hires many North Africans, to refer to work disguised as labor for the employer, but in fact diverted for one's own profit and pleasure. As time is money, the form this diversion invariably takes is time; time gets siphoned off and used for other free, creative alternative (profitable) activity. It may be as simple as stealing time to write a letter, or borrowing a tool to use at home overnight. Pleasure is derived by the very cunning in finding ways around the structured activity and in complicity with other workers, also conspiring to defeat the competition the factory tries to instill in them. The pleasure and profit is thus derived from putting one over on the establishment on its very home territory. De Certeau argues that far from being a regression toward an individual or tribal mode of production, *la perruque* introduces techniques from other times into the modern industrial space. Again, according to De Certeau, the activity of *la perruque* is analogous to readers or television viewers who privately consume books or shows for their own devices, for reasons seldom or never known by the cultural producers. In fact, the whole thing becomes one big game for which there are innumerable ways to foil the other's game (*jouer/déjouer le jeu de l'autre*), whereby the consumers continually evade their own consumption by those controlling the culture.

While De Certeau does not talk specifically about translation, the activity of translation seems well suited to illustrate his thinking. Certainly translation policies for popular political theatre come immediately to mind, how for example the San Francisco Mime Troop might stage Molière as opposed to a theatre in London's West End. The tactics of using the system for one's own ends can be seen most dramatically in translation under rigid systems of oppression, as in Russia or central Europe during the fifties to the late eighties. Pasternak, for example, censored for writing 'original' work, turned to translation – translating, for example, seemingly neutral Shakespearean sonnets – in order to say something else that could not be articulated within the dominant literary system at the time. All of the writers and most of the people read his translations and were able to read the otherwise dangerous political critique between the lines. It seemed as if only party officials were unaware of the processes of creative evasion at work. In fact, in many central European countries during this period, perhaps more creative work was going on through translation than through 'original' writing.

In fact, a study of translation along the lines of De Certeau's thinking may actually be more illuminating than some of Certeau's own examples, which are often drawn from monolingual and invisible spaces. For example, he makes certain claims about how an everyday reader reads, or how a TV viewer watches, activities that he has as little access to as any other cultural theorist. Yet if translation can be considered an act of reading, then such theorizing ceases to be speculative. Moving the study of translation to centre stage might be one way of documenting the invisible tracings of the practice of everyday life.

Translation and *The Fifties* in the USA

One of the most important poets, translators, and leaders of the counter-cultural movement during the sixties was Robert Bly. In 1966 he organized anti-war poetry readings at Reed College and the University of Washington and co-founded (with David Ray) American Writers Against the Vietnam War. Shortly afterward the group was staging readings all over the country, attracting the attention of national television and *The New York Times*. At the beginning there was much booing and hissing, and according to Bly, almost 90% of the audience opposed the readings. Along with Robert Lowell, Robert Creeley, and Denise Levertov, Bly became famous as an anti-war poet, and his poetry readings became counter-cultural events. His books *The Light Around the Body* (1967), winner of National Book Award in 1968, and *Sleepers Joining Hands* (1973) represent a shift in terms of the highly intelectual, metaphysical poetry characteristic in North America during the fifties, and moved the poet straight into the realm of politics and cultural policy. In his acceptance speech for the National Book award at the Lincoln Center, Bly gave the cheque for the prize to a representative of a group counselling draft resisters and went on to castigate the book industry and the Metropolitan Museum of Modern Art for their complicity with the war. How does one account for the radical shift in Bly's artistic development? How much did the literary centres contribute to his ideas and formation, as opposed to the counter-culture? And where, exactly, does Bly's literary translation fit in?

Like most of his generation, Bly was not raised in an avant-garde, counter-cultural environment. The son of a modest Minnesota farmer, he was educated in the public school system, attended Harvard University (1947–51), lived in New York City (1951–4), and attended the prestigious Iowa Writer's Workshop (1956). His early poetry, collected in anthologies such as *New Poets of England and America* (1957)[16] or published in his first book *Silence in the Snowy Fields* (1962),[17] tends to be lyrical, romantic and isolationist. The imagery of silence, snow and isolation reflect his solitary living experience in upstate Minnesota and alone in New York; there are few confrontational or political elements to be found. In 'Waking from

Sleep' Bly writes: 'Our whole body is like/a harbour at dawn'; in 'Poem in Three Parts' he writes: '[We] shall live forever,/like the dust'. In 'Silence' he writes: 'This new snow seems to speak of virgins'. While he was considered one of North America's new and upcoming poets, his early work reconfirmed established literary conventions and perpetuated existing forms and ideology.

What comprised the reigning literary centre at the time? At the very centre were the North American heavyweights; T.S. Eliot, Ezra Pound, Wallace Stevens, Marianne Moore and William Carlos Williams, still alive and writing their modernist poetry, yet hardly in the revolutionary spirit of the 1910s and 1920s. A reified, refined, conservative modernism reigned. Eliot had converted to Christianity, become a British citizen, and was writing things like, 'We cannot, in literature, anymore than in the rest of life, live in a perpetual state of revolution'.[18] He goes on to say that poetry should 'refine' rather than incorporate 'spoken language'. Ezra Pound had been tried for treason for his fascist radio broadcasts in support of Mussolini during World War II and been found insane, confined to St. Elizabeth's hospital where he continued to work on his modernist masterpiece *The Cantos*. Delmore Schwartz in *The Present State of Poetry* (1958) characterizes the period as a 'peaceful public park' on a Sunday afternoon, a cultivate suburban space separated from urban problems and polemics.

If anything could be characterized as 'new' during this period, it might be the 'New Criticism' as advocated by John Crowe Ransom, I.A. Richards, William Empson, Yvor Winters, Allen Tate, Cleanth Brooks, and, again, T.S. Eliot. The New Critics emphasized form over content, arguing that stylistic devices such as metaphor and rhythm had their own intrinsic meaning. The poem's value was derived from its formal qualities, especially by the poet's ability to combine disparate elements into a single unified whole, or in T.S. Eliot's words, 'heterogeneity compelled into unity by the operation of the poet's mind'.[19] Because extraliterary elements were considered ultimately irrelevant to a poem's value, biographical, cultural and historical formation were gradually elided from the interpretation and teaching of literature. According to new critical doctrine, 'good' poetry could be determined by aesthetic analysis, participated in a 'history' of formal and aesthetic development, and reflected universal, humanistic values that transcended time.

The leading journals supported this highly abstract, formal, and intellectual verse. Ransom edited the influential *Kenyon Review*; Harriet Monroe was still publishing *Poetry* magazine; John Ciardi edited the

Saturday Review; Howard Moss edited *The New Yorker.* Even more liberal
journals such as John Hollander's *Partisan Review* or Donald Hall's *Paris
Review* reinforced the literary hegemony. Younger poets seemed to
uncritically accept New Critical tenets. Contributors to the anthology
called *New Poets of England and America* (1957) included poets such as Bly,
Adrianne Rich, James Merril, W.S. Merwin, Richard Wilbur, Howard Moss,
William Meredith, all called the New Formalists at the time. While an
alternative scene existed, it too was highly intellectual, abstract, and
isolationist. Charles Olson's Black Mountain group, for example, which
began publishing in the early 1950s, in many ways complied with the
system in an abstract, transcendental, and highly intellectual fashion.

It is, in fact, in opposition to one of the Black Mountain school poets that
Bly articulates the position of his journal *The Fifties.* In the second issue
(1959), in an essay authored by Crunk (Bly) titled 'The Work of Robert
Creeley', we see that Bly is not fond of Creeley's work. Why? Because it is
too 'American' and too 'isolationist'. Bly argues thar Creeley's poems lack
images, that he does not go deep enough into himself. He also finds
Creeley's poems very abstract, concerned with neither oppression nor the
description of everyday life. Modern poetry, according to Bly, should
describe life using everyday speech, and be daring in its self-revelation.
And the subject matter should be the 'increasingly invisible oppression in
all countries'. Bly finds English and American poetry too intellectual (as
opposed to passionate), too suburban (vs. urban), too indifferent to
suffering (vs. compassionate). Bly finds North American verse rational and
sterile, verse that avoids the joys and traumas of the unconscious. It is
through the unconscious that deep images – the daring, the sensuousness,
and the savagery characteristic of Bly's version of modern poetry – can be
found. And for Bly, 'the poem *is* the images'.[20]

From where did Bly get this new, innovative, highly original (for North
America) aesthetic? Did it come from the centre of academia (Harvard), the
publishing capital of the country (New York), or most prestigious creative
writing programme (Iowa)? In fact, it derived from literary translation. In
1956 Bly received a Fulbright to translate Norwegian poetry into English
(he knew no Norwegian at the time; knowledge of foreign languages has
never been an important criterion for North American translators). It was
in a library in Oslo that Bly 'discovered' writers such as Juan Ramón
Jiménez, Pablo Neruda, Antonio Machado, Federico García Lorca, Gunnar
Ekelöf, and Georg Trakl. Finding new avenues to express his imagination,
Bly's days of solitude ended and he became an activist. When he returned
to the United States, he settled on a farm in Minnesota and, together with
William Duffy, started a new magazine called *The Fifties* in order to

articulate his differences with the prevailing literary standards. To do this he 'used' a variety of forms – authoring highly satirical and critical essays expressing his likes/dislikes, publishing poems by writers such as Louis Simpson, Denise Levertov and James Wright who expressed this new aesthetic, and creating fictitious awards such as 'The Order of the Blue Toad' parodying and exposing literary idols and critics. Yet perhaps the most influential vehicle he chose to combat the literary hegemony was to translate 'unknown' European poets.

The first issue of *The Fifties* (1958) contained translations of Swedish poems by Gunner Ekelöf, Danish poems by Tom Kristensen, and French poems by Henri Michaux. Bly also published work by American poets Donald Hall, Gary Snyder, and W.D. Snodgrass, and included an essay on 'Five Decades of American Poetry' in which he argued that the 'new imagination' first appeared in the 1910s with writers such as Eliot, Pound, Williams in the USA, Apollinaire and St. John Perse in France, Saba and Ungaretti in Italy, and Trakl and Benn in Germany. Bly wonders, however, what happened to it in North America and argues that the poets translated in *The Fifties* demonstrate that Europeans such as Ekelöf, René Char, and Michaux have carried on, making contributions to the 'new imagination', while North America lost it. He asks why more North American poets do not write of despair, of the Second World War, of business experience, of filling stations, of mass deaths in trenches. He concludes his summary of the last fifty years of American poetry by saying we need more poets who can 'carry on a sustained raid into modern life'.[21]

The first Spanish poet to turn up in *The Fifties* is Juan Ramón Jiménez, a selection of whose poetry was translated by Carlos de Francisco Zea. It appeared in the second issue (1959). Of all the Spanish poets of the generation of '98, Jiménez was perhaps the most unknown in North America, all the more ironic since he had lived most of his life in the United States and Puerto Rico since going into exile in 1916, and had married the sister of a man who owned a Spanish-American newspaper in New York. At the time he won the Nobel prize for literature in 1956, not a book of his had been published or translated in the United States. Why was Bly attracted to Jiménez, a poet whose work today seems at first sight slightly simplistic and sentimental? Jiménez' work could hardly be characterized as subversive or political. Yet for all his simplicity, Jiménez was a very complex poet. Poetry for him was not merely a form of writing, but a kind of religion, a path, a way to salvation, and above all, an 'ecstasy' of love. It is this emotion, or in Jiménez' words 'naked poetry', that attracted Bly. The term derives from Jiménez' famous untitled poem from 1918 that begins *'Vino, primero, pura,/vestida de inocencia . . .'* [She came at first pure/clothed in innocence']. The poem tells the story of how poetry came to him first as a naked young girl, whom he loved; later, as she grew older, she clothed herself and put on jewelry, and he began to feel bitterness. Finally, as she went back again to her old innocence, he believed in her again. The poem ends with *'Oh, pasión de mi vida, poesía/desnuda, mía para siempre'* ['Oh, passion of my life, naked/poetry, mine forever'].[22] Bly is also attracted to the precision of Jiménez' short poems: in just a few words Jiménez can evoke the most powerful feelings.

'Naked poetry' also refers to the use of direct everyday speech, to the lack of adornment, of elaboration. Jiménez' poems are non-egotistical according to Bly, not complicated by long complex stanza forms or involuted syntax. The first poem included in the second issue of *The Fifties* opens *'Intelijencia, dame/el nombre exacto de las cosas! . . . Que mi palabra sea/la cosa misma'* [Intelligence, give me/The exact name of things!/ . . . Let my word be/The thing itself'].[23] Bly thus uses Jiménez to attack North American poetry's intellectualism, its pontificating, its elevated forms, and its abstract language. According to Bly, Creeley and some of the West Coast poets are no different than those highly intellectual university poets. In an essay entitled 'On English and American Poetry', Bly writes, 'Many of the poems in the quarterlies of the West are a blizzard of abstract words – no different in that respect from those in the *Kenyon Review'*.[24] Jiménez thus opens a way for Bly to explore emotions, to articulate one's pleasures, one's anxieties, to explore the 'deep images of the unconscious'. At the same time Bly uses Jiménez to advocate a candid direct style, one that anyone can understand.

In the fourth issue of his journal, now called *The Sixties*, Bly continues to develop an aesthetic he calls the 'new style' or the 'new imagination'. The poem by Mexican poet Enrique González Martínez, translated by Bly, served as a kind of manifesto: *'Tuércele el cuello al cisne de engañoso plumaje/que da su nota blanca al azul de la fuente;/él pasea su gracia no más, pero no siente/el alma de las cosas ni la voz del paisaje'* ['Take his swan with puffy plumage, and wring its neck,/Who gives his white touch to the blue of the fountain pool;/He displays his elegance only, but does not understand/The soul of creatures, or the voice of the silent fields'].[25] The swan here represents all those North American poets writing beautiful, abstract, well-crafted poems that are out of touch with everyday lives of everyday people. In this issue, Bly 'introduced' the Spanish poets Antonio Machado and García Lorca. In 'A Note on Antonio Machado' Bly argues that North American poets are more sensitive to ideas and intellectual formulations and prone to use words such as 'distinction', 'natural', 'time', and 'mortality'. Spanish poets, on the other hand, are more sensitive to words such as 'owls', 'sea', 'night', and 'darkness'. 'In the intellectual world of Marianne Moore, which is the world of all American poetry today, we try to bring the real owls into the imaginary orchard of the poem, but Machado does not do that. He brings the poem to the owl'.[26] In the poems collected, Machado writes about ordinary life – about people crying, church bells ringing, castle walls crumbling, squalid alleys, dogs howling, crows cawing, and the aroma of bean plants. Not mere descriptions, these poems are charged with emotion, often joyful feelings. As with Jiménez, these translations of Machado by Bly and Willis Barnstone are among the first to be published in the United States.

The simple life for Machado was also a noble one: Machado himself lived most of his life in small towns in the mountains, taking long walks in the towns and hills. It was this proximity to simple life that actually allowed Machado to avoid intellectual formulations and to listen to his inner self. In the same issue, Bly translated and published a note Machado wrote to a 1917 reissue of his early poems *Soledades* (first published 1903) to help explain Machado's aesthetic. Machado wrote, 'The substance of poetry does not lie in the sound of the word, nor in its color, nor in the poetic line, nor in a complex of sensation, but in the pulse of the depth of the spirit; and this deep pulse is what the soul contributes . . .'[27] Machado continues to argue that the poet ought to 'overtake by surprise' some of his own conversations with himself, to try to record the 'vigorous images' that might help express one's deepest feelings. Bly was attracted to the objective description of ordinary life combined with the expression of deep personal emotion. He used Machado's texts to lobby for simple, often colloquial language, to strive for clear meanings, to direct one's work to everyday people – which also meant not being afraid to criticize oppressive political and systemic structures. In a way he was using the fame of Machado, and the brilliance of his poems, to lend authority to a style of writing that otherwise might easily have been dismissed by the literary editors, teachers and critics in the United States.

In contrast to Jiménez and Machado, García Lorca was well-known in the United States as a writer and dramatist. *Poeta en Nueva York,* written about his experience in New York City at Columbia in 1929–30 was published in Spain in 1940 and immediately translated by Rolfe Humphries. Stephen Spender had translated García Lorca's poems as early as 1939; by 1951 Langston Hughes had translated Lorca's *Gypsy Ballads*; and at least two editions of his plays translated by James Graham-Lujan and Richard L. O'Connell had appeared by the mid-fifties. Lorca's murder by Franco partisans in 1936 had also contributed to his international fame. In his essay on Lorca and René Char, Bly asks how France produces a Char, how Spain produces a Lorca, while in America, after a dry flurry of leftist writers during the thirties, poetry seems to be getting older every year, 'like a running down clock'.[28] Bly answers his own question by arguing that in Eliot and Pound, the mind won over the unconscious, 'an old Puritan victory'. Nevertheless, Bly argues that it is possible to write poetry other than intellectual verse, and that Spanish poetry seems a strong avenue to opening up a revolutionary poetry of the unconscious.

Similar to Jiménez' concept of 'naked poetry' or Machado's sense of the 'deep pulse', Bly is attracted to Lorca's ability to find images to tap into the unconscious feelings of ordinary people, what Lorca has referred to as 'cante jondo' ['deep song'] or 'pan moreno' ['brown bread']. Bly publishes, for example, James Wright's translation of a short poem titled 'August...' with lines like 'La panocha guarda intacta,/su risa amarilla y dura./Agosto./Los niños comen/pan moreno y rica luna' ['The ear of corn keeps/Its laughter intact, yellow and firm/August./The little boys eat/Brown bread and rich moon'.[29] The images of brown bread and rich moon tap into certain elemental, sensuous emotions that all people – children, workers, old folks, seem to share. While on the one hand they are 'modern' images, carrying on a European tradition started in the 1910s, they are also tempered by another tradition – a folk tradition passed down in oral cultures in fables and ballads. Politics inescapably creeps in. In an excerpt from Cante Jondo translated by J.A. Cottonwood, Lorca writes about the comings and goings in a simple tavern: 'La muerte/entra y sale/de la taberna./Pasan caballos negros/y gente siniestra/por los hondos caminos/de la guitarra' ['Death/Is entering and leaving/The tavern./Black horses and dark/People are riding/Over the deep roads/Of the guitar].[30] Whether 'dark' conveys the mood of 'siniestra' is another question. The tone, the fear, the oppression are nevertheless conveyed. And while the emphasis is on content and mood, the unspoken inner anxiety is present, and the style remains unembellished, simple and direct.

Bly and Duffy continue this strategy of using translations to influence and change the North American literary establishment throughout the sixties. In subsequent issues of The Sixties, translations by writers like the Chilean poet Pablo Neruda and the Peruvian poet César Vallejo appear. Bly calls for the use of increasingly graphic imagery to convey deeply felt emotions and comes to think more clearly about the connections between inner feelings and outward political poetry. Bly also becomes increasingly aware of how schools, churches, TV, and museums are used by the state to smother the awareness of the American people. It perhaps should come as no surprise to translation scholars that Bly found it difficult to publish his own poetry during this period. One book, For the Ascension of J.P. Morgan, considered too political for the Eisenhower fifties, remains unpublished to this day. Bly's first published book was *Twenty Poems of Georg Trakl* (1961), translated by Bly and James Wright. In Bly's case, translation as a tool for changing the literary establishment in a 'strong' literary system might be viewed as indispensable, certainly for his own future career. Later, in the sixties, Bly's own work began to see the light of day. While *Silence in the Snowy Fields* (1962) may reflect his living experience in upstate Minnesota and alone in New York City more than his confrontation with political oppression in Spain, there are some exceptions. In the disturbing, complex poem 'Unrest', echoes of Lorca and Machado can be heard. 'A strange unrest hovers over the nation/This is the last dance, the wild tossing of Morgan's seas'. This unrest is more specifically articulated in Bly's 1967 collection *Light Around the Body*. Here Bly critiques the cultural trend in the USA toward increased consumerism, dependency upon the automobile, fast foods, and disposable items. This critique culminates in the middle section of the book, which contains perhaps the best known anti-war poem of the decade, 'The Vietnam War'. Far from writing a simple, political propaganda piece, Bly connects the war to spreading American capitalism, suggesting that capitalism's inherent need for new markets has pushed the Western frontier of America all the way to Asia. In the lead poem of the section titled 'After the Industrial Revolution, All Things Happen at Once' Bly writes 'I saw a black angel in Washington dancing/On a barge, saying, Let us now divide kennel dogs and hunting dogs; Henry Cabot Lodge, in New York,/Talking of sugar cane in Cuba; Ford,/In Detroit, drinking mother's milk . . . And Wilson saying, 'What is good for General Motors . . ./Who is it singing?'[31]

Of interest is not just Bly's politics, but his use of language to subvert official versions being spread by mainstream sources. First, Bly uses the language of the bureaucrats and their advertising agencies and turns it against them, parodying their voices. Secondly, he interrupts their language with surreal images, as in the following excerpt from 'The Teeth Mother Naked at Last', first published by City Lights Books in 1970 and later collected in *Sleepers Joining Hands*:[32]

> *'From the political point of view, democratic institutions are being built in Vietnam, wouldn't you agree?'*
>
> A green parrot shudders under the fingernails.
> Blood jumps in the pocket.
> The scream lashes like a tail.
>
> *'Let us not be deterred from our task by the voices of dissent . . . '*

The whiteness of the jets
pierce like a long needle.

As soon as the President finishes his press conference, black
wings carry off the words,
bits of flesh still clinging to them.

A kind of European black humour is involved, as Bly is pointing fun at white America's language and logic. A philosophical point was also being made, one perceived by several writers who covered the war. To what does the language used by those disseminating information about the war refer? What is real, what is not real? The government officials have one version of reality, which they try to make stick; but what is its relation to the 'truth'? Some journalists called news briefings by the military in Vietnam 'the five o'clock follies'. Yet very few knew what was really going on. Often those in the war characterized the death and destruction witnessed as surreal, the escape into pop music and consumerism as real: 'When are you going back to the 'real' world?'

From where did Bly develop a repertoire of devices for dealing with such a situation? Not only do I contend that the repertoire was developed through doing literary translations; in addition I argue that he *used* translations to change the system, to break down dangerously meta-physical thinking and moralizing attitudes, in order to create cultural conditions to allow his verse to appear. His use of translations undermined elitist notions about the nature of art, its unity and form, and helped open a space for poets to talk about the dirty world of politics and everyday life. Bly's work ushered in a new generation of poets, and marked the beginning of the end of formalist, high modernist verse. Eliot's 'objective correlative' was successfully replaced by a simpler, yet none the less powerful, form of imaging, an image that is not out there in the world, but called up from within. Confessional poetry – W.D. Snodgrass, Anne Sexton, Sylvia Plath – emerged. Poets sympathetic to Bly's spirit, or at least interested in uncovering certain unconscious but powerful emotions – Donald Hall, James Wright, Galway Kinnell, Louis Simpson – began successfully publishing. The form of poetry advocated invariably referred to a world accessible to ordinary people and their lives. Being a poet became simpler; simple; everybody has their own 'psychic rhythms'. Anybody, Bly once argued, could sit down and write a poem. The idea was popular, and when these poets read, audiences came. Perhaps most interestingly, a whole new generation of translators was spawned, for the European and Latin American writers seemed ahead of the North Americans in accessing these inner psychic rhythms, often had more direct experience of oppression and problems involving basic survival, and had found styles that used the language of the oppressor to their own advantage. The 1960s boom in literary translation, however, has its roots in the earlier decade.

Thus Bly's emergent style is not simply one of the protest and confrontation, but one which engages and evades, subverting old forms and creating new ones. Bly's work in translation during the fifties played an important role in the development of the new form of poetry. His translation work also led to a very creative and highly invigorating period not just in Bly's verse, but also in his *life*. During this period, Bly moved to the forefront of an anti-establishment movement (anti-academic system, anti-literary centres, and anti-war), and his case supports the thesis that translations played a key role in causing the ensuing cultural crisis. Only after Bly had already found alternative styles via translation was he able to creatively disrupt the system from within in his own work.

Conclusion

While the 1950s in the US may be represented as a fairly unified and normative culture for study, it is actually a complex period in which subtle forces are at work. While historians and sociologists make generalizations about the conservative and uncritical nature of the general population at this time, I suggest that such generalizations may obscure important cultural events. Does Marilyn Monroe conform to the norms of Hollywood or represent a cultural misfit? What does the brooding silence of a James Dean represent? Why does Rosa Parks sit down on a different place on a bus? Translation during this period is equally complex, and seems to refuse sublation into normative trends. Why does Langston Hughes translate Lorca before most white Americans have heard of him? Why is Bly reading Spanish poets in the library at Oslo? What is Merwin doing in the mountains of Spain and Portugal, translating oral tales told by medieval *juglares* and passed on in ballad/oral form for centuries? Why is Denise Levertov hitchhiking all over France with an American GI? What is Ferlinghetti doing hitchhiking through Mexico, or living in a basement in Montparnasse? While Ferlinghetti and the beats represent a distinctly 'American' voice now at the root of much popular culture in the States today, his 'surreal verses', carnivalesque images and vivid playfulness in *Coney Island of the Mind* (1956) have more to do with Latin American modernism and French existentialism than anything 'inherently' North American or 'originating' in Anglo-American literary centres.

To the ps-theorists, I suggest that not nearly enough data have been collected to make such sweeping generalizations about literary translation as a conservative force. The former Soviet Union, once postulated by ps-theorists as enjoying a 'strong' literary polysystem – and clearly the early post-World War II Israeli system imported many styles and genres from Soviet models – perhaps today appears less so. Questions with regard to how translations functioned in the Soviet system remain today. What was said between the lines, and how were translations 'read' by consumers? Many translations may have enjoyed a double life – consumed by party supporters in one fashion, but read by others in a distinctly different fashion. Certainly the subversive and radical use of literary translations in many former 'East-bloc' nations is beginning to emerge.

While the use of a cultural studies model such as Michel de Certeau's may immediately lend itself to the analysis of highly repressive cultural systems such as the former Soviet Union, I also suggest its usefulness in analyzing the role translations play in the development of culture in the 'democratic' system of the United States. Art and literature in the United States does not function in the same manner as in many West European nations. Bly points this out in an interview published in *Talking All Morning* (1980). In responding to a question about the relationship between government and art, Bly refers to the subculture, suggesting that in European countries like Sweden, for example, culture is hierarchical, and poetry feeds into a cultural system that leads right up to government. In the United States, however, there is another culture, not really touched by that hierarchy (see epigraph above) that behaves in a spontaneous, noncommercial and politically alive fashion.[33] If indeed the polysystem in the United States differs so radically from western European cultures, how might literary systems in the developing world differ? Clearly much more research needs to be done before laws of translational (and transnational) behaviour can be formulated.

Notes

1. Robert Bly and William Duffy (eds) (1958–60), *The Fifties (The Sixties)*, issues 1–4.
2. Cf. Itamar Even-Zohar, *Papers in Historical Poetics* (Tel Aviv: Institute for Poetics and Semiotics, 1978); *Polysystem Studies, Poetics Today* 11, 1, 1990. Gideon Toury, *In Search of a Theory of Translation* (Tel Aviv: The Porter Institute for Poetics and Semiotics, 1980); and 'What are Descriptive Studies into Translation Likely to Yield apart from Isolated Descriptions?', in Kitty M. van Leuven-Zwart and Ton Naaijkens (eds), *Translation Studies: The State of the Art* (Amsterdam: Rodopi, 1991).
3. Even-Zohar, *Papers in Historical Poetics*, p. 53.
4. *Ibid.*, p. 24.
5. *Ibid.*, p. 25.
6. Cf. Annie Brisset, 'In Search of a Target Language: The Politics of Theatre Translation in Quebec', *Target* 1, 1 (1989), pp. 9–28.

7. *Ibid.*, p. 17.
8. *Ibid.*, p. 25.
9. *Id.*
10. Toury, 'What are Descriptive Studies into Translation Likely to Yield Apart from Isolated Descriptions' in *Translation Studies: The State of the Art*, p. 186.
11. *Ibid.*, p. 189.
12. Michel de Certeau, *The Practice of Everyday Life*, trans. Steven Rendell (Berkeley: University of California Press, 1984), p. xii.
13. *Ibid.*, p. xviii.
14. Trans. Brian Massumi. (Minneapolis: University of Minnesota Press, 1986).
15. Cf. *Id.*
16. Donald Hall, Robert Pack and Louis Simpson (eds), *New Poets of England and America* (Cleveland: Meredian Books, 1957).
17. Middletown, CN: Wesleyan University Press, 1962.
18. Quoted in Elliot Emory (ed.), *Columbia Literary History* (New York: Columbia University Press, 1988), p. 1080.
19. Quoted in Alex Preminger and T.V.F. Brogan (eds), *Princeton Encyclopedia of Poetry and Poetics* (Princeton: Princeton University Press, 1993).
20. Emphasis in original, *The Fifties*, 1959, p. 14.
21. *The Fifties*, 1958, p. 39.
22. See *The Fifties* 2, 1959, pp. 54–5.
23. *Ibid.*, p. 24.
24. *Ibid.*, p. 46.
25. *The Sixties* 4, 1960, p. 2.
26. *Ibid.*, p. 14.
27. *Ibid.*, p. 15.
28. *Ibid.*, p. 7.
29. *The Fifties*, 1960, p. 25.
30. *Ibid.*, p. 21.
31. Robert Bly, *The Light Around the Body* (New York: Harper and Row, 1967), p. 29.
32. New York: Harper and Row, 1973.
33. Robert Bly, *Talking All Morning* (Ann Arbor: University of Michigan Press, 1980), p. 28.

8 Translation and Canon Formation: Nine Decades of Drama in the United States

ANDRÉ LEFEVERE

The basic premise of this essay is that a translation of a literary work is one way of rewriting a literary text. Other types of rewriting literary texts are the compilation of anthologies, the production of literary criticism and literary history, and the editing of texts. These types are listed, and the rationale for listing them is explained more extensively in my *Translation, Rewriting, and the Manipulation of Literary Fame*.[1] Some of these rewritings merely refer to the texts they rewrite, as when titles and short plot summaries of literary works are mentioned in literary histories. Other rewritings reproduce the texts they rewrite to some extent, as when comic strip, or some movie versions of literary texts succeed in mainly reproducing the plot lines of their originals. Still other rewritings claim to represent the texts they are rewriting. Translation in the more traditional understanding of the word would be a prime example of this category. In fact, prospective readers who walk into most bookstores in the United States wanting to buy Brecht's *Mother Courage*, will only be able to buy the English translation/rewriting of that play, since the original is likely to be available only in a very select number of specialized bookstores. If they do not have German, and if they are not familiar with German literature, they will not mind this at all. They will, in fact, read the translation, the rewriting, as if it was the original text, and they will experience this state of affairs as normal, leaving professional readers of literature, such as critics and theoreticians, to agonize over it.

The way in which a translation is made therefore does matter enormously for readers who need translations because they cannot read originals. This is all the more ironic because translations are usually judged and criticized by those who are able to compare them with their originals and therefore, by definition, do not need translations at all. The way in which translations are produced matters because translations represent their originals for readers who cannot read those originals. In other words: translations create the 'image' of the original for readers who have no access to the 'reality' of that original. Needless to say, that image may be rather different from the reality in question, not necessarily, or even primarily because translators maliciously set out to distort that reality, but because they produce their translations under certain constraints peculiar to the culture they are members of. These constraints may be ideological in nature, as when most translations of the classics of Greek and Roman antiquity produced in the nineteenth century either omitted passages then considered 'obscene' altogether, or rendered passages of that type found in Greek originals into Latin in the translations, and passages of that type found in Latin originals into Italian in the translations. These constraints may also be poetological in nature, as when Homer and Virgil were translated into prose in the fifties of this century because the epic had been pronounced dead and it was widely believed that readers would only want to read novels from then on. The fact that Homer and Virgil are now routinely translated into verse again is as good an indication as any of the much more important fact that these constraints are by no means eternal and unchangeable; rather, they, too, are subject to changes in the socio-cultural environment in which translations and their originals are produced. Finally, these constraints may be of an obvious economic nature, as when a third of the songs were cut from the Broadway production of Brecht's *Mother Courage* because the play would otherwise have been classified as a musical by the Broadway unions, and the production costs would have increased accordingly.

If a translation provides its readers with an image of its original, another type of rewriting, often produced to meet more obviously didactic goals, namely the compilation of anthologies, tries to provide its readers/ students with an image of a literature, a period in a literature, a type, such as drama in general, as opposed to narrative prose, for instance, or the lyric, and a genre, a subdivision of a type, such as Brechtian epic theatre, for instance, as part of the more encompassing concept of drama. If anthologies contain translations, they provide their readers with a double image. There is a macro-image the anthology as a whole tries to project, and the micro-images different translations collected in the anthologies project in their turn. We realize the importance of these images as soon as we wake up to the fact – and those of us who are professionally engaged with the study of literature are usually not too quick to do this – that these anthologies are the vehicle by means of which non-professional readers, not just the proverbial (wo)man in the street, but also students on the High School and University level who have no intention of becoming professional readers of literature, make literature's acquaintance in the first (and last) place.

Anthologies of drama of the type that will be discussed here are used in the US High Schools and Universities to introduce students to the evolution of the genre from the Greeks to the present. Students who do not go on to study literature will be left with these images for the rest of their lives. For them, the texts put together between the covers of these anthologies represent the canon of drama (or poetry, or the novel, or what have you). Or perhaps it would be closer to the truth to say that these anthologies try to pass themselves off as the canon to readers who read them either for educational purposes or to satisfy an interest or a curiosity. The power wielded by these anthologies is therefore not to be underestimated (and neither is the power wielded by individual translations). And yet these (and other) rewritings are hardly studied or analyzed at all. They are simply taken for granted, they seem to remain invisible, as if the 'spirit' or what have you of the original passes through them to the reader by means of some undefined process of osmosis. These (and other) rewritings have to be taken for granted, they have to remain transparent, if the main premise of much of literary studies since Romanticism is to be kept alive, that is, if the writer, touched by genius, is to speak to his or her fellow (wo)men directly, out of the fullness of his or her emotions, even if he or she speaks another language altogether. By contrast, learned tomes have been written, and continue to be written about canons and canon formation, without touching once on what I propose to discuss in what follows: the hidden makers of what to many people does indeed become a living canon, and their agendas, hidden or otherwise.

I shall try to illustrate the points made above by a brief and (very) preliminary analysis of the corpus of drama anthologies published in the United States between 1900 and 1988. One of the earliest anthologists, Brandon Matthews, who will be introduced here as representative, in many ways, of those who were to follow in his footsteps, very definitely defines himself as a maker of canons in the introduction to his *The Chief European Dramatists*, published in 1916:

> Hitherto, however, no adequate attempt has been made to select, out
> of the drama of the remoter past and out of the drama of other tongues
> than English, a group of plays, tragic or comic, which might illustrate

and illuminate the development of dramatic literature from the Greek of the fifth century BC to the Scandinavian at the end of the nineteenth century AD.[2]

Having described the task he set himself, Matthews goes on to list the difficulties he had to cope with in trying to carry out that task:

It has been his duty to ascertain who, among the scores and the hundreds of playwrights that have flourished in the different countries of Europe during the past twenty-four centuries, were entitled to be recognized as acknowledged masters of the art of the drama or as indisputable representatives of their race and of their era.[3]

Some characteristic features of these two statements will be found in many, if not all subsequent introductions. The anthologist has to assume the burden of selection. Interestingly enough, the corollary to this is almost never discussed, namely: on what authority does the anthologist shoulder this burden? My contention is that this point is never discussed because the answer to the question would not quite match the lofty tone prevalent in the statement quoted above and in other, similar statements made later. That answer is likely to be that the authority in question is not conferred by any muse or other vaguely angelic and allegorical figure, but rather by publishers trying to tap into what they think is likely to be a lucrative market. Anthologies like the ones under discussion here were and are aimed at both the college market and the interested individual. Even in 1916 the college market must not have been negligible and it has, of course, grown more than exponentially by 1988 and beyond.

If we accept the premise that it is really the publisher who confers the mantle of authority, we must also accept that the framework within which makers of canons make their selection is delimited by factors other than just excellence and/or considerations of a pedagogical nature. That framework is also delimited by the number of pages the publisher is willing to invest in any given anthology, and those numbers of pages are closely tied to the hours of course work required by institutions of (higher) learning. The basic framework may, therefore, well turn out to be that of the semester or year of study, in which a number of playwrights/plays need to be 'done', and which does not allow for much, if any time over and beyond that number.

If this is true, it should become obvious that the semester framework also allows for relatively little in the field of radical change. It is not easy to suddenly bring an anthology on the market that doubles the number of selections, for instance. Rather, it would appear as if a (more than) relatively finite number of niches has been reserved for select playwrights and plays, a number that corresponds to the alloted class time per semester or year, so that for a new playwright or play to occupy a given niche its previous occupant will have to vacate it. The same holds true for genres, not just in the 'fundamental' opposition between such basic types as comedy and tragedy, but also in the differentiation between historical drama, bourgeois drama, drawing room comedy, and other genres that have developed throughout the history of drama.

If most of the anthologies under discussion here are indeed aimed at the education market, the margin for competition among these anthologies will be relatively small, and room for innovation will be limited accordingly. As a result – and this is also the reason why so much attention is devoted here to an anthology published in 1916 – the first anthology to enter the market is likely to set the tone for the many others to come. The first anthology, it could be said, delimits the parameters within which further anthologies can be put together, since different institutions of higher learning cannot be seen to be teaching wildly different selections under the same course heading likely to read 'Introduction to Drama'.

As a result, the anthologies under discussion here will – and do – display an inbuilt weighting toward the conservative. It is not easy to introduce new playwrights and/or plays, or even new translations: Archer's translations of Ibsen only definitively disappear from these anthologies as late as the 1950s. Add to this that it is not always easy to find translations of plays recognized as new and important within their own cultures; this mere fact of literary life creates a time-lag that can delay the inclusion of new plays and their authors in anthologies by a number of years, or even a decade. That anthologies are weighted toward the conservative end of the scale is already obvious in the following statement also made by Matthews' introduction: 'The principles of dramatic art are unchanging through the ages, the same today in Paris or in New York that they were in Athens twenty-four hundred years ago'.[4]

These principles tend to be equated mainly with the concept of genre, as practiced by the 'masters of the art' referred to by Matthews above. The problem for the anthologists then becomes which genres to include and which to leave out, or even whether to recognize new genres, such as Brecht's epic theatre, or the plays of Pirandello. In fact, many anthologists did not do so until the early sixties. Overall, anthologists appear to be more comfortable with the genres they consider 'established', such as the classical and neo-classical tragedy, and the nineteenth century 'well-made play', which developed out of the bourgeois drama of the eighteenth century. Not infrequently the uneasy coexistence between the established and the new gives rise to formulations so cautious that they get perilously close to the grotesque, as in the introduction to Johnson, Bierman, & Hart's *The Play and the Reader*: 'We have reserved the special problems of Pirandello's philosophical drama, of Brecht's 'epic' theatre, and of the Theatre of the Absurd, represented by Max Frisch, to the end of the volume'.[5] It should be added, of course, that Frisch was, and is, not really associated with the Theatre of the Absurd, at least not within the framework of German language theatre, or the wider framework of European theatre as a whole.

Finally, the anthologist has to also solve the problem of which playwrights to recognize as 'indisputable representatives of their race and of their era'. Matthews includes one play by Aeschylus, Sophocles, and Euripides, thereby establishing a classical Greek trinity that will return in a fair number, though by no means in most of the anthologies put together by most of his successors. He also includes Aristophanes' *The Frogs*, in the translation made by John Hookham Frere about a hundred years before, but his successors did not follow him in this, for obvious ideological reasons: many of Aristophanes' plays were considered 'obscene' and therefore either not included in most anthologies, or included only in an expurgated form. Matthews also includes one play by Plautus and one by Terence. Subsequent anthologists settle for one Roman comedy writer only, not two. Medieval theatre is conspicuously absent in Matthews' anthology, and the historical thread is taken up again with one play each by Lope de Vega and Calderón. In many subsequent anthologies, the theatre of the Spanish Baroque was to receive much less attention. Matthews further includes one play each by Corneille, Molière, and Racine, introducing another trinity, but one that is not likely to reappear in most subsequent anthologies, which tend to prefer Racine to Corneille, making Racine, in effect, the 'token' French neo-classical dramatist. Many anthologies also tend to include Molière more often than they exclude him. Moving along chronologically, French theatre is heavily represented with Beaumarchais, Hugo, Alexandre Dumas fils, and a play called *The Son-in-Law of M. Poirier*, written by the now obscure team of playwrights Augier and Sandeau.

The appearance of this play raises the question of the possible incorporation of contemporary, or near-contemporary plays into the canon, arguably the area in which the room for 'mistakes' is the greatest. Many subsequent anthologists also include playwrights or plays that were popular at the time the anthologies were published, but vanished from subsequent anthologies, never to return.

Strangely enough, Matthews' anthology ends by including not only Goldoni, after Alexandre Dumas fils, thus interrupting, for no apparent reason, the chronological sequence observed until then, but also one play each by Lessing, Goethe, Schiller, Holberg, and Ibsen. Matthews' selection seems to suggest that the 'true', or rather, the dominant tradition of the European theatre is the French one, at least since neo-classical times, with the Italians, Germans, and Scandinavians somehow tacked on. This, too, is a pattern that does not altogether disappear until the 1950s, and can be said to live on in an attenuated form even later. The reason for this may well be that French plays in translation were incorporated into the British repertoire at a much earlier date than other European plays. In his influential 1933 anthology, *World Drama*, about which more later, Barrett H. Clark, for instance, includes a 1793 translation of Molière's *Le bourgeois gentilhomme*, entitled *The Cit Turned Gentleman*. The problem of the 'universality' of the canon is thus raised time and again, but never resolved. Certain national traditions are definitely privileged above others. Some, predominantly non-Western, are hardly ever included, or even considered for inclusion, presumably because trying to include them would make for too great a discrepancy between competing anthologies at any given time. This fact again reinforces the impression one has of the power, not only of institutions as such (of higher learning and others), but also, maybe even more predominantly so, of the inertia of those institutions as a significant factor constraining the anthologists' selections.

A chronological survey of the anthologies published between 1900 and 1988 illustrates the problems referred to above. The problem of the niches filled and/or vacated by authors is perhaps best illustrated by the fate of the Danish dramatist Holberg: he appears in 1916 and 1933, and never again thereafter. In terms of including or excluding, or even recognizing different genres, the historical play disappears after 1939. Schiller's *Wilhelm Tell* appears in 1916, 1933, and 1939; Goethe's *Goetz von Berlichingen* appears in 1916 only, and his *Egmont* in 1933 only. Victor Hugo's *Hernani* also appears only in 1916 and 1933. No other historical plays appear in any of the anthologies surveyed here. The bourgeois comedy suffers a similar fate: Lessing's *Mina von Barnhelm* appears in 1916 and 1933, as does Beaumarchais' *The Marriage of Figaro*. No other representatives of the genre appear in any anthology published during the time-frame adhered to in this essay.

In terms of the choice of authors considered representative for a certain 'era', to use Matthews' words again, the Roman comedy writer Terence only appears in 1916, 1933, 1946, and 1957. All other anthologies prefer Plautus instead. Conversely, Sophocles is most often the token Greek classical dramatist, being left out only in 1944, 1953, and 1961. Aeschylus and Euripides, on the other hand, are left out about twenty times each in the period surveyed here. In the same vein Racine is obviously the token French neo-classicist dramatist: he appears in virtually all anthologies published between 1900 and 1988, whereas Corneille only appears in 1916 and 1933. Also in terms of 'eras' and 'races', to speak with Matthews one last time, all medieval plays, where they appear in the anthologies at all, are English, except for the French *Master Patelin* in 1933 and 1939, the French *Adam* in 1933, the Latin *Quem Quaeritis* in 1927, and the German *The Wandering Scholar* in 1933.

As mentioned above, inclusion of all 'races' never seems to have been even a remote objective in the composition of drama anthologies, most of which silently identify 'drama' with 'Western drama'. In fact, non-Western plays are only included in three anthologies: five in 1933, one in 1957 and again one in 1964. It should be added that the 1933 anthology which included five non-Western plays, B.H. Clark's *World Drama*[6], in two volumes, was published as the drama anthology to end all drama anthologies, not least because its publisher had obviously decided to allow for more choice by almost doubling the number of plays usually included. Clark's anthology did not supersede all others, but it was definitely considered to be in a class of its own, and its influence made itself felt well into the fifties, and some would argue, even beyond. It probably represents the most extensive attempt at creating a canon to be found in any of the anthologies analyzed here. It contains the four Greek dramatists – Menander had not yet been rediscovered in 1933 – the three Latin ones (Clark is among the very few to include a play by Seneca), five medieval plays (*Adam, The Second Shepherd's Play, The Farce of Worthy Master Pierre Patelin, Everyman*, and even the German playwright Hans Sachs' *The Wandering Scholar from Paradise*). The Jacobeans are represented with three plays, as are the Restoration dramatists. The Italian eighteenth century is represented not only by Goldoni, but also by Beoleo, Scala, and Alfieri. Spain's Golden Age is represented by Cervantes, Lope de Vega, and Calderón. The French drama of the neo-classical era and beyond is represented by Corneille, Molière, Racine, Beaumarchais, Hugo, Alexandre Dumas fils, but also the enigmatic Augier and Sandeau which, incidentally, also raises the problem of filiation: do certain anthologists include certain plays simply because they are to be found in other anthologies, and are therefore easily accessible in translation? This problem becomes even more acute, as has been touched on above, when 'new' playwrights and plays are to be included. The plays usually exist in one translation only, which is then dutifully included in many subsequent anthologies, more often than not for lack of an alternative. German drama is represented with Lessing, Goethe, and Schiller; Holberg and Ibsen represent Scandinavia, and Russian drama is included by means of an Ostrovsky play. But most significant of all, Clark's anthology also includes *Sakoontala*, *The Chalk Circle*, an anonymous Japanese play called *Abstraction*, Seami's *Nakamitsu*, and Chikamatsu's *Four Ladies at a Game of Poem Cards*. The five non-Western plays, grouped together here to emphasize the point I am making, are fully integrated into the chronological unfolding of the development of what can here truly be called 'World Drama'. No other anthology under discussion here can stake the same claim, which is a further reminder, if one were needed, of the extent to which the canon of 'drama' has remained Euro-centric, in the sense that it has been limited to the drama of Europe and its historical dependencies.

Obvious lacunas in Clark's anthology are Strindberg, who is not represented at all, and O'Neill. In the latter case it might conceivably be argued that O'Neill could still, in 1933, be regarded as not 'fully established', or, at any rate, not established enough to merit a place among the classics of all time. It would be more difficult to make the same argument for Strindberg, however. The absence of both Strindberg and O'Neill must, therefore, in my opinion, be regarded as much more symptomatic of tenacious reluctance to include plays that do not conform to either the (neo)classical or the well-made play muster. The canon, it seems, must be limited to the categories just mentioned, even though certain compromises with 'the other side' are occasionally made, no doubt under the pressure of that side's popularity at any given time, which remains the barometer for inclusion or exclusion. The most striking observation, in this context, is that no dramatist who can be regarded as belonging to 'the other side' has managed to permanently occupy a niche in the anthologies published since 1933, nor has any single non-well made play established itself to the extent of Molière's *Tartuffe*, for instance, or Sophocles' *Oedipus the King*. Strindberg himself enters the anthologies with *Miss Julie* in 1939, which is again included in anthologies published in 1967, 1970, and 1988, but not between 1939 and 1967. Strindberg's *The Father* appears in anthologies in 1940 and 1957, and not before or since. *The Ghost Sonata* is included only once, in 1961, as is *The Dance of Death*, in 1962. Finally, Strindberg's *The Stranger* makes two appearances, one in 1970 and in 1973, whereas *There Are Crimes and Crimes* appears once only, in 1957. It is no exaggeration to conclude, therefore, that neither Strindberg nor one of his plays managed to establish himself/itself as part of the canon of what is regarded as drama by those in the United States who saw it as their task to educate the theatre-going audience to appreciate excellence.

Similar fates have befallen three other writers often associated with the avant-garde in drama. Pirandello enters the anthologies in 1940, with *Six Characters in Search of an Author*, is dropped until 1946 for what must have been mainly ideological reasons at the time, and reappears, often with the same play, in 1957, 1964, 1968, 1970, 1971, 1972, and 1973. Yet, he disappears completely after 1973, whereas it could be argued convincingly, to my mind, that he should have established himself as a 'modern classic' by the sixties, or definitely by the seventies. Not that his plays were performed all the time during those decades, but neither were those of Plautus or Racine, for instance, whereas the latter two are usually represented in anthologies published after 1973.

Brecht enters the anthologies in 1961, about twenty years later than Pirandello, presumably because the ideological resistance he had to overcome was much greater. Significantly, he is also most often represented with plays that can be interpreted as having 'least' to do with Marxism. *The Private Life of the Master Race*, included in a 1957 anthology, can easily be read as primarily a satire on Nazi Germany. *Mother Courage*, included only in 1968 and 1970 can, by means of a judicious introduction and a few equally judicious 'interventions' in the translation, easily be turned into a 'tragic' figure in the more or less classical mode, whereas *The Good Woman of Setzuan*, included in 1961, 1967, and 1972, can just as easily be transformed into a parable. This is exactly what happened to both plays in Eric Bentley's translations, which are, not surprisingly, the translations used by the anthologies under discussion here. All the more surprising, therefore, that *The Caucasian Chalk Circle* should have been included four times, in 1967, 1970, 1971, and 1972, although even in this case it can be argued that the audience may well be counted on to remember the 'actual' play much more than the introductory and concluding scenes framing it. Because of their position in the original, these scenes can also easily be downplayed, or even dropped in translation.

Ionesco appears for the first time in 1961, with *The Lesson*. *Maid to Marry* follows in 1967, *The Leader* also in 1967, and *The Gap* in 1972. A greater surprise where non-well made plays are concerned is that Dürrenmatt, Frisch, and Adamov only appear once each, Dürrenmatt in 1961, with *The Visit*, Frisch in 1971 with *The Firebugs*, and Adamov in 1972 with *Professor Tarane*. The greatest surprise of all in this context is undoubtedly that Beckett is only included three times, with *Happy Days* in 1968, and again in 1988, and with *Act Without Words I* (admittedly no great sacrifice in terms of the investment to be made in terms of pages) in 1967. Although it can be argued that *Waiting for Godot* drastically changed the course of drama from the sixties onward, readers of these anthologies would have to gather this information from other sources.

The anthologies under discussion here are not only fundamentally conservative in terms of poetics, that is in terms of how they define (good) drama; they are equally conservative in terms of ideology. Not only does Marxism never really make it beyond the fringes, and if then, only in a much watered-down version, thoughtfully packaged by means of introductions and notes, but Ibsen's *Ghosts*, arguably not the least important of his plays, is never included at all, undoubtedly on account of its subject matter. No doubt Aristophanes' *Lysistrata* is only included twice in almost ninety years for the same reason. Significantly, the rise of feminism, also in the field of literary theory and criticism, seems to have been virtually powerless to influence selection in the Greek comedy writer's favour.

If the selections in most of the anthologies under discussion here are conservative in both ideology and poetics, they also tend to be conservative in that they favour two national traditions, the English, because that is the most obvious one for the readership aimed at, and the French, partially because, of the other national traditions, the French was the one that established itself first on the English stage, and partially because of the American fascination with things French and the peculiar identification of 'high culture' with whatever is (or can be made to sound) French. The discrepancy between the treatment meted out to the French and the German traditions, no doubt also reinforced (twice) in the course of the century by ideological reasons, is striking: Goethe's *Faust*, not exactly an unimportant piece of dramatic art, nor an obscure one, is only included twice, first in 1900, and then not again until 1957, probably also because quite a few anthologies include a more 'native', though fundamentally different treatment of the same theme, namely Marlowe's *Dr. Faustus*. Of the other German-language inclusions, over and beyond Brecht, Dürrenmatt, and Frisch, Hauptmann's *The Assumption of Hannele* (1927), can be interpreted as something approaching a medieval allegorical play, and *The Weavers* (1940, 1957) is a well made play in structure, if not in diction. Hebbel's *Maria Magdalena* would also still fit the category of the well made play, which may be the reason why it appears three times, thereby surpassing Goethe, namely in 1940, 1946, 1953, and 1957. Georg Kaiser's *From Morn to Midnight* appears in 1962, and then again in 1967, at a time when interest in the dramatist and his works had already waned in Germany. Kaiser may have been included as an ideologically more palatable alternative to Brecht, even though in poetological terms his work is as far removed from the well made play muster as that of his one time rival. Büchner also makes two appearances, one with *Danton's Death* in

1957, and one with *Woyzeck* in 1972. Whether Büchner appears 'in his own right', meaning as a playwright who wrote his novel plays in isolation, or as a 'representative' of German Expressionism, and a more famous one than Kaiser at that, is hard to say. Finally, the lone appearance of Wedekind's *The Tenor* in 1957 is a reminder of the very important fact that no discussion of anthologies like the present one can afford to ignore personal idiosyncrasies on the part of anthologists, who might either like a play so much that they want to include it at all costs, or who might include certain plays, no more than a sprinkling compared to the solidly conservative/traditional choices, as part of a very cautious attempt, always subject to abrupt termination at the publishers' displeasure, to extend the boundaries of the canon somewhat.

The fact that the great majority of these anthologies were designed to serve as textbooks for classroom teaching, goes a long way towards explaining the fundamental and tenacious conservatism underlying the selections, both in terms of ideology (no ethically objectionable or potentially subversive subject matter) and poetics (no, or definitely not too many, experimental plays whose presence might disturb the tax payers, who are, in their great majority, arguably not professional readers of literature, because they would not strike said tax payers as immediately intelligible). In the introduction to their 1927 anthology Hubbel and Beatty even take care to appease the tax payer on another score, when they state: 'For the inclusion and discussion of foreign plays we have no apology',[7] implying that the 1927 US audience, whose insularity was admittedly even greater then than it is now, might expect such an apology after all. Hubbel & Beatty's introduction is further remarkable for the fact that it is not overtly didactic. Their statement 'the chief purpose of every writer of plays is to give pleasure to the spectators who come to his plays; and the spectators come primarily to be amused',[8] stands in marked contrast to the statements made in other introductions. Yet they, too, produce a statement that could be found in other, more avowedly didactic introductions: 'The permanent and the temporary conventions need to be clearly distinguished for they are easily confused'.[9] About forty years later, Small & Sutton agree that:

> though each culture, each reader, and even the same reader at different times, reads a literary work differently, knowledge of what can be factually known about it and its times is a protection against an anarchic subjectivity of interpretation that could eventually destroy its continuum of identity.[10]

This pedagogically motivated desire for clarity and order shines through most obviously in the introduction Hogan & Molin wrote in 1962: 'The audiences that fill the theatres, however, are not especially informed ones'. The anthologists, therefore, see it as their task to overcome the 'critical cleavage that reflects the absence of a theatrical heritage and experience'[11] admittedly by the most conservative of means: since 'the ideas of genre today are confused and confusing', Hogan & Molin resort to 'an Aristotelian notion of genres' to provide 'a key to understanding and judgment'.[12] In other words, Aristotle's poetics are still seen as the 'true' yardstick against which all subsequent drama is to be measured, not least for pedagogical purposes. Aristotle becomes the venerable name, elevated above all suspicion, used to justify the underlying conservative tenor of most selections in most anthologies, even if that tenor is occasionally masked by means of a 'folksy' style in statements like 'trying to hazard a definition is like trying to grab a bowl of jello'.[13]

Yet the conservatism of the anthologies must still be packaged in such a way that it appeals to both students and the general reader. The most obvious way to do this is to topicalize the past. Perhaps the most extreme formulation of this strategy is to be found in Alice Venezky Griffin's introduction to Plautus' *Mostellaria* in her 1953 anthology *Living Theater*. She rightly wants to point out Plautus' contribution to the development of drama, and does so by stating that 'Plautus was the Rodgers & Hammerstein of his day'.[14] Millet & Bentley state essentially the same in their introduction to Plautus in their own 1933 anthology, *The Play's the Thing*: 'Perhaps his most notable innovation (unobservable in the translation of his works) is the development of lyrical passages and of recitatives to be intoned or chanted to the accompaniment of the flute'.[15] The ways in which the two statements are expressed could not be more different. Millet & Bentley admit that Plautus' main contribution is lost in translation anyway, whereas Alice Venezky Griffin appeals to readers' and students' imagination by putting Plautus' text squarely into a tradition they are thought to be familiar with: that of the musical. She goes on to say that 'just as *Oklahoma* greatly influenced the pattern of American musical comedy, so the works of the Greek comedy playwright, Menander, became a model for the Roman dramatists'.[16]

The topicalization strategy (as opposed to a strategy that would leave Plautus 'untouched' in his own time, and translate his texts into a diction associated with that of the classics over the years: slightly archaic, slightly dull, and heavily footnoted) can also be found in the actual translations included in the anthologies under discussion. I shall round off this essay by briefly comparing two translations of Plautus' *Mostellaria*, one by Lynn

Boal Mitchell in the Alice Venezky Griffin anthology mentioned, and one by A.S. Downer in his own anthology, *Great World Theater* published about thirty years later.[17]

Mitchell, as befits a translator translating for an anthology entitled *Living Theater*, is more radical in trying to turn Plautus into a writer of well made plays, and she wants to put him in the Shavian tradition. She therefore adds stage directions like the following at the beginning of Scene 3:

> In front of the house of Theopropides are disclosed a table provided with boxes for jewelry, cosmetics, perfumes, manicurist's buffer, etc. There are two couches near the table, on the one farthest from Philolaches sits Philematum. Scaphia stands behind her, arranging her hair.[18]

The stage direction, which is not there at all in the original, anchors the translation in the tradition of the drawing room comedy, and more specifically in its Shavian variant because of its length and the profusion of objects mentioned in it. The translation also tries to keep the punning of the original. Downer professes to do the same justifying his practice in a rather defensive footnote: 'For those readers who (unlike the translator) detest puns, it should be pointed out that here, too, the English text attempts to be conscientious'.[19] Maybe he felt he had to apologize for trying to be 'clever', or maybe he wanted to counteract the audience's tendency not to associate puns with Romans. Neither translator is too successful, though, in trying to render the pun in *'detexit, tectus qua fui'* (line 163 in the Loeb Classical Library edition,[20] which translates *Mostellaria* as *'The Haunted House'*), likening the beloved to a storm that uncovered, but also tore off the roof where the lover was covered/roofed, to such an extent that he *'neque iam umquam optigere possum'* (line 164), will never be able to re-cover/re-roof again. Mitchell writes: 'That rainstorm which unroofed me . . . Nor can I now repair the damages'.[21] Downer tries: 'Ripped off the roof of modesty . . . too late to repair it'.[22] Both are more successful in rendering line 257: *'Nunc adsentatrix scelesta est, dudum adversatrix erat'*, something like: 'Now the wicked woman is a "consentress", who was an adversary until now'. Downer writes: 'Is now a Yes-woman, a minute ago she was a No-woman'.[23] Mitchell renders: 'She was a 'No-No-er', now she is a 'Yes-Yes-er'.[24] When it comes to translating *'Te ille deseret aetate et satietate'* (line 196), something like 'He will desert you because of your age and his satiety', though, Downer tries 'when you're dated and he is sated'[25] to render the Latin opposition *'aetate et satietate'*, whereas Mitchell simply writes 'when his love's grown cold',[26] thereby missing a Shavian opportunity.

Throughout, Mitchell tries to make Plautus' text correspond to the image of Rome and things Roman she suspects her prospective readers to have. When the *order 'capiundas crines'* (line 226) is given, something like 'fix up your hair', Downer translates: 'put your hair up',[27] but Mitchell makes the heroine 'wear orange blossoms for him',[28] no doubt because Roman girls are often portrayed in paintings and sculptures wearing blossoms in their hair. For the same reason Mitchell adds another stage direction at the end of this scene. In that stage direction she lets Philolaches, the heroine's master and lover, treat Sphaerio, another slave, as follows: 'Sphaerio . . . kneels. Philolaches washes his hands and dries them on Sphaerio's hair'.[29] In doing so, Mitchell evokes shades of Sienkiewicz, Bulwer Lytton, and other writers of popular historical novels dealing with ancient Rome, who offered their readers at least one such scene per book. Downer adds nothing here, preferring to leave his Plautus closer to the original, or trusting more in his readers' imaginative powers.

Mitchell is also closer to Shaw in diction; Plautus' *'lepida'* (line 170) becomes 'deucedly smart' in her translation,[30] whereas in Downer the heroine 'merely' 'knows a bag of tricks'.[31] Mitchell further tries to make Plautus' diction more directly accessible, or at least she tries to translate in such a way that the dialogue affects the audience more directly. When the master/lover has set his slave girl/beloved free, that slave girl's servant and former fellow slave makes the following observation: *'ille te nisi amavit ultro/id pro tuo capite quod dedit perdiderit tantum argenti'* (lines 210–11). The Latin means something like: 'unless he [your master/lover] will love you beyond this [or: go on loving you], he will have lost all that money that he gave for your head'. Mitchell translates: 'He is hanging around to be repaid for the money he invested in your freedom'.[32] The audience obviously does not have to decipher here; Downer translates much more literally, and lets the audience do more of the thinking work. When Mitchell later translates the master/lover's statement: *'quae pro me causam diceret, patronum liberavi'* (line 244), something like 'I have freed a lawyer who will plead my cause', she adds 'I have an Athena to defend me',[33] obviously banking on the 'name recognition' a name like 'Athena' will bring. Downer does not do anything of the kind.

Topicalization may be taking Mitchell too far when she translates the Latin *'meretricium'* (line 190), something like 'mistress', by 'Geisha'.[34] The ensuing 'culture clash' may well be too great if one thinks of the most obvious, Japanese meaning of the word 'geisha', without reducing it to its other, second accepted meaning of 'courtesan'. Attempts at 'acculturating' the Latin sometimes lead both translators astray. When Plautus has one character tell another: *'accumbe'* (line 308), something like 'lie down', because the Romans did, after all, eat lying down, Mitchell uses the somewhat vague, and also, in the context, somewhat disconcerting: 'take your place',[35] whereas Downer simply translates 'sit down',[36] certainly de-romanizing Plautus while possibly making him more acceptable to the audience likely to read the translation.

Both translators feel the necessity to expand on Plautus' line 289: '*pulchra mulier nuda erit quam purpurata pulchrior*', something like 'a beautiful woman will be more beautiful naked than dressed in purple'. Downer adds: 'ornament doesn't do much good if natural charm is lacking. Women who are unattractive only spoil beautiful clothing. And if they're beautiful they need no ornament'.[37] Mitchell goes even further and adds: 'For the lover of a Geisha buys favors with gold and purple . . . Purple is fit for hiding old age, and gold is for an ugly woman (to take one's thoughts off her looks) . . . Besides, she loves her pains in togging herself out, if she has a mean disposition'.[38] It is rather doubtful whether the audience learns more from Downer's elaboration than from the original text, whereas Mitchell, not satisfied with making the woman old, proceeds to make her spiteful as well, a transformation for which there is no warrant in Plautus, though there is in much popular lore.

Yet there is no point in trying to construct the opposition between the two translations in stringent terms: both Downer and Mitchell are, after all, people of flesh and blood who translate not just according to a strategy, but also according to their own idiosyncrasies. Consider their translations of lines 304 and 305. The Latin reads: '*Bene igitur ratio accepti atque expensi inter nos convenit;/tu me amas, ergo te amo; merito id fieri uterque existimat*'. A translation might read: 'The ratio of what is taken in and what is paid out fits well among us;/you love me, therefore I love you; we both think that is how it should be'. Mitchell translates: 'You love me (that is a receipt): I love you (that is a disbursement. The two are identical in amount)',[39] capturing the mercantile metaphor. Downer gives the lines a Shakespearean ring, perhaps prompted by the fact that they are to be found close to the end of the scene, by translating: 'our credit and debits thus balance precisely;/Your love and my love pair off very nicely',[40] the kind of translation one would have expected from Mitchell, whereas Mitchell's translation would seem better suited to Downer, and yet both translations are precisely where they are, presumably because Mitchell is Mitchell and Downer is Downer.

It is perhaps wise to end this essay with a caveat about its underlying methodology, which should definitely not be applied in a mechanistic way. Yet this caveat by no means detracts from the basic premise underlying what goes before: the great, yet hidden power wielded by those who rewrite literature, as opposed to those who write it, and the vital necessity to investigate what precisely happens in the process of rewriting, why, and what image of a text, a literature, a genre rewritings project, and why.

Notes

1. André Lefevere, *Translation, Rewriting, and the Manipulation of Literary Fame* (London and New York: Routledge, 1992).
2. B. Matthews (ed.), *The Chief European Dramatists* (Boston: Houghton Mifflin, 1916), p. ix.
3. *Id.*
4. *Ibid.*, p. x.
5. Stanley Johnson, Judah Bierman and James Hart (eds), *The Play and the Reader* (Englewood Cliffs: Prentice Hall, 1971), p. xi.
6. B.H. Clark (ed.), *World Drama* (New York: Dover Publications, 1993).
7. Jay B. Hubbel and John O. Beatty (eds.), *An Introduction to Drama* (New York: Macmillan, 1927), p. vii.
8. *Ibid.*, p. 1.
9. *Ibid.*, p. 16.
10. Norman M. Small and Maurice L. Sutton, *The Making of Drama. Idea and Performance* (Boston: Holbrook Press Inc., 1972), p. 4.
11. Robert Hogan and Sven Eric Molin (eds), *Drama: The Major Genres* (New York and Toronto: Dodd, Mead, and Company, 1962), p. xiii.
12. *Ibid.*, p. xiv.
13. Small and Sutton, *op. cit.*, p. x.
14. Alice Venezky Griffin (ed.), *Living Theater* (New York: Twayne, 1953), p. 85.
15. Fred B. Millet and Gerald Eades Bentley (eds), *The Play's the Thing* (New York and London: D. Appleton-Century Company, 1933), p. 161a.
16. A.V. Griffin, *op. cit.*, p. 85.
17. Alan S. Downer (ed.), *Great World Theater* (New York: Harper and Row, 1964).
18. *Living Theater*, p. 90a.
19. A.S. Downer, *op. cit.*, p. 88.
20. Paul Nixon (ed. and trans.), *Plautus*, vol. 3 (London: Heinemann and New York: G.P. Putnam's, 1924. The Loeb Classical Library).
21. Mitchell, *apud* Griffin, *op. cit.*, p. 90a.
22. Downer, *op. cit.*, p. 95.
23. *Ibid.*, p. 97.
24. *Apud* Griffin, *op. cit.*, p. 92a.
25. Downer, *op. cit.*, p. 96.
26. *Apud* Griffin, *op. cit.*, p. 91a.
27. Downer, *op. cit.*, p. 97.
28. *Apud* Griffin, *op. cit.*, p. 91b.
29. *Ibid.*, p. 93a.
30. *Ibid.*, p. 90b.
31. Downer, *op. cit.*, p. 95.
32. *Apud* Griffin, *op. cit.*, p. 91a.
33. *Ibid.*, p. 92a.
34. *Ibid.*, p. 90b.

35. *Ibid.*, p. 91b.
36. Downer, *op. cit.*, p. 99.
37. *Ibid.*, p. 98.
38. Mitchell *apud* Griffin, *op. cit.*, pp. 92b/93a.
39. *Ibid.*, p. 93a.
40. Downer, *op. cit.*, p. 99.

Notes on Contributors

Susan Bassnett is Professor of Comparative Literature at the University of Warwick and head of the Centre for British and Comparative Cultural Studies. Her most important publications include *Translation Studies* (1980, 1991) and *Comparative Literature* (1993). She has also co-edited, with André Lefevere, *Translation, History and Culture* (1992). She has taught throughout the world and written extensively in the fields of comparative literary studies, theatre, cultural studies, women's studies and translation studies. She is a practising translator.

Theo Hermans edited in 1985 his well-known anthology entitled *The Manipulation of Literature*. He is the author of numerous articles on translation theory. He teaches at the University College of London.

Javier Franco is a freelance translator. He also teaches on the Master's Degree Course in Translation Studies, University of Alicante (Spain).

Ovidio Carbonell teaches translation theory at the Faculty of Translation, University of Salamanca. He has written articles on translation and post-colonial studies.

Enrique Alcaraz is head of the Department of English Studies, University of Alicante, and Director of a Master's Degree in Translation Studies. He has lectured on translation in London and Brussels, and has written several books on linguistics, pragmatics and translation: *Tres paradigmas de la investigación lingüística* (1991), *El inglés jurídico* (1994), and others. He is the author of an English-Spanish/Spanish-English Dictionary of Legal English.

Edwin Gentzler is the author of *Contemporary Translation Theories* (Routledge, 1993). He teaches in the Department of Comparative Literature at the University of Massachusetts/Amherst.

André Lefevere (1945–1996) was Professor in the Department of Germanic Languages, University of Texas at Austin, and Honorary Professor of Translation Studies at the University of Warwick. His principal publications include *Literary Knowledge: A Polemical and Programmatic Essay on its Nature, Growth, Relevance and Transmission* (1977), *Translating Literature: The*

German Tradition (1977), *Translating Poetry: Seven Strategies and a Blueprint* (1975), *The Tradition of Literary Translation in Western Europe: A Reader* (1991), *Translation/History/Culture: A Sourcebook* (1992), *Translation, Rewriting and the Manipulation of Literary Fame* (1992), *Translating Literature: Practice and Theory in a Comparative Literature Context* (1992).

Román Álvarez teaches at the University of Salamanca, where he was head of the Department of English for six years, and is now Director of the British Council Office in Salamanca. He has published books and essays on diverse aspects of English literature, and for ten years has co-edited the journal *Anglo-American Studies*. His latest publications include an anthology on Postmodernism and a collection of essays on comparative (British-Spanish) cultural studies.

M. Carmen-África Vidal teaches at the Faculty of Translation (University of Salamanca, Spain). She has written a book on translation studies (*Traducción, Manipulación, Desconstrucción*, 1995), and some others on critical theory: *¿Qué es el posmodernismo?* (1989), *Hacia una patafísica de la esperanza* (1990), *Pintura posmoderna española* (1991), *Arte y literatura: Interrelaciones entre la pintura y la literatura del siglo XX* (1992), *Futuro anterior: Reflexiones filológicas sobre el fin de siglo* (1994). She is co-editor of *Abanicos excéntricos: ensayos sobre la mujer en la cultura posmoderna* (1993) and of *Postmodernism: A Global Issue* (1995). She has also translated 12 books from English into Spanish and numerous articles.